3 95

Date Due

OCT 20 82			
FEB 6 84			
MAY 26 86			
FEB 29 '92			
MAR 06 '92			
NOV 26 '92			
DEC 10 '92			
FEB 19 '93			

CAT. NO 24 162   PRINTED IN U.S.A.   BRO DART

D1383525

INTERNATIONAL LIBRARY

WALLY HERBERT

ESKIMOS

COLLINS · PUBLISHERS   FRANKLIN WATTS, INC.

Glasgow · London · Toronto   New York

First Edition 1976 (U.K.)
Second impression 1978
First published in the United States
of America by Franklin Watts Inc. in 1977

ISBN 0 00 100177 9 *(Collins cased edition)*
ISBN 0 00 103368 9 *(Collins paperback edition)*
SBN 531 02124 6   *(Watts cased edition)*

CONTENTS

CHAPTER ONE

ESKIMO
PREHISTORY

North America, like the rest of the Northern Hemisphere, went through at least four major glacial stages during the Pleistocene. The last of these, which in America is known as the *Wisconsin*, dates roughly between 90,000 and 10,000 years ago. It may itself be subdivided into several cold climatic phases, or stadials, each of which was followed by a warmer interstadial.

Now the extent of the ice cover during the individual phases of the Wisconsin is not yet certain. It is, however, generally believed that some parts of Alaska remained ice free even during the period between 23,000 and 13,000 years ago when the ice sheet surged to its maximum extent and buried the whole of Canada (see Fig. 1). So much water was evaporated from the sea and deposited as snow on the high lands and ice caps that the sea level during this period sank by some 90 to 100 metres (300 to 330 feet). Coastlines changed. Asia became linked with Alaska in the area now known as the Bering Sea, opening up the route for animals moving eastwards across the Arctic in search of new grazing and for men in pursuit of game.

But this "bridge" was not one isolated event in geologic history. Sea levels and ice caps interact as part of the dynamic of climatic change and, according to some scientists, the Bering "bridge" formed then flooded at least twice during the Wisconsin: the first forming sometime around 40,000 years ago; the second, linking the two continents between 28,000 and 10,000 years ago. The extent of the ice cover between 23,000 and 13,000 years ago when it was at its maximum, however, blocked all routes between the ice-free areas of Alaska and the ice-free areas to the south of the ice sheet. It would seem, therefore, that there were only three periods when animals and men could have made the journey from Asia to America unhindered by ice or water: sometime about 40,000 years ago; sometime between 28,000 and 23,000 years ago, or from 13,000 to 10,000 (Fig. 1).

This is not to say that all migrations from Asia to America ceased each time the connection between the two continents was broken by a rise in sea level. Even today the distance between Siberia and Alaska is only about 80 kilometres (50 miles), and it must at times have been much less; but since the crossing would have been a hazardous one because of the current that rips through that Strait (and which would have flowed even faster when the Strait was narrower), we may presume that the Bering Strait put a stop to all but the most determined hunters whose way it barred.

In the whole evolution of mankind there has not been a race of men or a single cultural element more distinctive than that phenomenon which we call Eskimo.

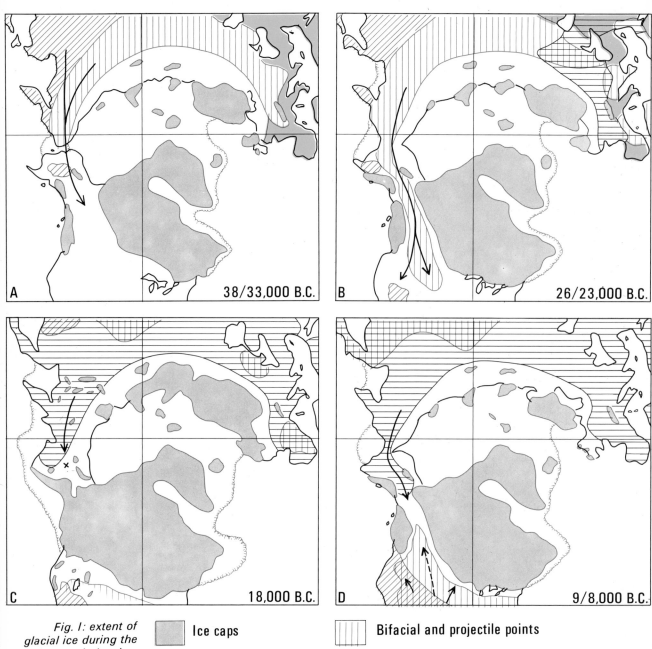

A   38/33,000 B.C.

B   26/23,000 B.C.

C   18,000 B.C.

D   9/8,000 B.C.

Fig. I: extent of glacial ice during the three periods when man might have crossed the "bridge" from Asia on to the American Continent.

After H. Muller-Beck 1966 and Hans-Georg Bandi 1969.

▨   Ice caps

■   Mousteroid industries

▨   Pebble tool industries

▥   Bifacial and projectile points

▤   Aurignacoid industries

⩚   Limit of Summer Ice

The first Americans

We know very little about man's earliest struggles, nor is it possible to tell from his fossilized remains at what stage in his development he learned to communicate with words. But we do know from what has been dug up in Africa that he learned to hunt, became carnivorous and, in search of meat, wandered so far from his homeland that by the time he had reached that stage in his development when he was able to make a variety of simple tools (about 50,000 years ago), Stone Age man had appeared on all continents except the Americas and of course Antarctica.

Some prehistorians believe that the first human beings to arrive on the American Continent were of the "archaic" white stock that had been widespread before mankind split up into three races: the white-, black- and yellow-skinned groups. So far, however, archaeologists have produced no proof that the earliest migrations from Asia to America took place at the time of the "first" Bering "bridge" (see Fig. 1a). For of the many sites and objects found

headed south after crossing the Bering "bridge" to escape the hostile climate, to search for better hunting territories, or were pushed south by the waves of men that bore down on them from behind, we cannot say for certain; but the fact that no trace has yet been found in Alaska of any human settlements dating back to that "second" infiltration suggests that these immigrants must have dispersed rapidly from that congested area "to get out of the way", and once clear of Alaska, kept on wandering until they had populated every habitable tract of the continent right down to the southernmost tip of Tierra del Fuego.

Only the Eskimo regarded the winter as his dominant season and the sea with its treacherous skin of ice as his "natural" element.

in North, Central and South America, which have been tentatively dated at between 30,000 and 40,000 years old on account of their primitive form, none as yet have been confirmed either stratigraphically or by radiocarbon dating. There is, on the other hand, ample evidence of a later semi-Mongoloid infiltration into America, which many scholars argue must have come by way of the Bering "bridge" that existed between 28,000 and 23,000 years ago (Fig. 1b).

Whether these early immigrants

There are indications that some groups intermingled with people of an "archaic" white stock (which lends support to the theory of an earlier infiltration). Such a mixing of blood would account for the many and various types of Indians and Amerindians, some of whom (like the Incas, Aztecs and Mayans) were to reach a very high level of civilization before being overrun by the Spanish in relatively recent times. There are indications too that some groups made their way north again at the end of the Ice Age

to hunt in the regions that were now becoming ice-free, and that these so-called "Palaeo-Indian" groups, who had by this time developed a specialized and fairly advanced hunting technique, came into contact with tribes who had been part of the third and last infiltration from Asia (Fig. 1d).

These last immigrants, who had arrived sometime between 13,000 and 10,000 years ago, were almost pure Mongoloid—an arctic people whose isolation and continual struggle to stay alive had weeded out all the weaker elements of their physical structure, leaving them short in stature with small, strong hands, tiny feet and flat, narrow-eyed faces with skin as smooth and as dark as planed teak. They came through, however, not as a result of these slight evolutionary changes in their physical form—changes brought about by that same rigorous process of natural selection by which *any* animal is capable of adapting to a new environment providing the change is neither too sudden nor too extreme—for their physical and metabolic adaptation was, in evolutionary terms no more than a token adjustment of the human species to an environment in which it was ill-equipped to live. Their survival, more likely, was due to the fact that their implements,

though crude, were adequate, and their hunting technique, though primitive, more often than not was effective.

But it would be a mistake to call these people Eskimos merely on account of their physical characteristics, for the climate along the arctic coast at about the time of this "third" infiltration was much milder than it is today. The tundra was a lush carpet of vegetation with thickets of dwarf willows which were good feeding grounds for game—and game there was in abundance. They hunted mammoth and musk-oxen. They competed with the packs of wolves for caribou and mountain sheep. They snared birds, collected eggs and fished the rivers in summer, and at the beginning of each dark winter returned to their dens to feed sparingly on their stores of meat and "hibernate" till spring.

But if, as it is generally believed, they were culturally no further advanced than the Ice Age hunters who had roamed the tundra of northern Europe some 30,000 to 40,000 years ago at what stage did they become Eskimo? According to the anthropologists, the origin of any new culture is not the development of those separate elements which distinguish it from a neighbouring group, but the synthesis of those elements which, in the case of the

Eskimos, was their adaptation to the sea.

It is, of course, no more likely that these Stone Age hunters abandoned their old hunting grounds out of choice than that they moved from the interior to the coast from some perverse preference for a harder and more hazardous way of life, for if there is one thing all primitive people have in common, it is their fear of the unfamiliar. The fact is, they *had* no choice. The mammoths died out, the muskoxen and caribou migrated south into the territory of Indian tribes, leaving these hunters with but one alternative to extinction as a race—to change, to adapt to a new environment and develop a specialized hunting technique to survive in that part of the world where no other men could live.

The inspired guess

The problem with any attempt to trace the early stages in the adaptation of those hunters to the sea is that one cannot dig into the subject of Eskimo prehistory without getting lost among books and learned papers full of questionable dates, anomalies and half-formed facts. Look for chronology and all you will find is confusion. Look at the picture the prehistorians are trying to put together and all you will find are a few odd pieces of a puzzle, most of which still lie scattered over an area of more than two million square miles either buried beneath the sub-soil or exposed but as yet undiscovered on the terraces and beaches along the arctic coast. But if, to the archaeologists' dilemma of where to start digging, you add the cost and the problem of getting to the Arctic and the frustration of having to fit each field programme into that 100-day period between the summer thaw and the first

sharp frost of autumn, then it seems hardly surprising that the "inspired guess" in this subject is accepted as a perfectly legitimate way of filling in the gaps between each rare and often doubtful point of reference.

For example: the artefacts found in 1947 at a site in Brønlund Fjord in north-east Greenland on a terrace some twelve metres (forty feet) above sea level which have reliably been dated at 4,680 years old, bear a striking resemblance to finds made in 1948 at Cape Denbigh in Alaska ascribed to the period between 5,000 and 4,500 years ago—and yet, these two sites are at least 8,000 kilometres (5,000 miles) apart and there is no evidence from either site that these people made use of the dog. A link, nevertheless, was immediately made between the two, and the finds said to corroborate the theory that these two groups were related—the slight differences in the style of the artefacts being neatly accounted for as alterations which would naturally have come about during the course of a long migration or as "the divergent characteristics of individual craftsmen". Now what is more significant than the ease with which these conclusions were reached is that when the discovery was made of other sites along that 8,000-kilometre (5,000-mile) route which pointed to an error in the original theory, it was not the new evidence itself that destroyed it, but the "inspired guess" by which that new evidence was reshuffled to form a different pattern.

And this is going on all the time. Every archaeologist has his own theories and any attempt to summarize the whole confused subject of Eskimo prehistory is simply asking for trouble. It seems to me, however, that there are a few threads

This walrus ivory figure known as the "Okvik Madonna" (which is only about 16 centimetres [6½ inches] high) came from the Okvik site on Punuk Island near St Lawrence Island in the Bering Strait. Small carvings of human figures are a characteristic of the Okvik culture and some, such as this one of a woman holding a small animal in her hands, are thought to have served as idols or auxiliary spirits which were on the side of the hunter.

From a drawing by the author.

in this unravelled rope that are stronger than the rest, and if we take it that they can be traced back to those who crossed the Bering "bridge" sometime between 13,000 and 10,000 years ago, then a picture accurate enough for our present needs will surely begin to take shape.

The Proto-Eskimo

One characteristic of primitive people is that they always took the easiest routes, and since there is no reason to believe that the hunters who crossed the Bering "bridge" from Siberia to Alaska were the exception to the rule, we may assume they made their way into the interior not at that point where today the gap between the two continents is narrowest, for there the coastline is too rugged; but more likely a little further south up the river valleys of the Yukon and Kuskokwim, and to the north up the Kobuk valley (Fig. 2).

From there they spread out as all hunters must—to make space. And

not in one wave, but several. Some moved east across the Canadian Arctic, while others, penetrating the sub-arctic barrens, came into contact with Palaeo-Indians by whom they were influenced and with whom they may even have intermingled. But there are still many gaps in our knowledge, for traces of these early migrations are few and far between. We do not know when they set out or when they reached their furthest point east on the shores of Hudson Bay. Nor do we know whether these isolated groups gradually adapted to the sea, or whether the first people to reach north-east Greenland were one of the many new cultural waves which spread eastwards from Alaska.

The latter at first glance seems the more likely, for it would account for the sudden appearance at several locations throughout the Arctic of a culture distinctly "Eskimo" in character. But track those migrations to their source on the shores of the Bering Sea in the hope of retracing the development of this

Fig. 2: The Bering "bridge" and the probable routes taken by the migrating tribes from Asia on to the American Continent.

Archaeological sites dated between 6000–8000 BC marked by triangles; sites dating between 2000–6000 BC marked by circles.

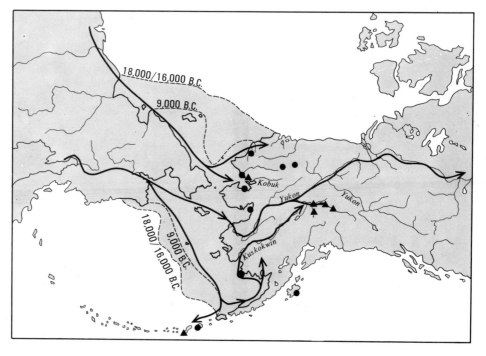

culture back deep into the past, and you will find yourself in the year 4000 BC at the edge of a black chasm 5,000 years wide—a cultural gap on the far side of which lived a race of primitive men.

Here on Alaska's north-west coast and on our side of that gap in time, we are among the Denbigh seal hunters—the first in a long line which can be followed without a break right through to the Thule people, the most advanced hunting culture the world has ever seen, and it is but one short step from them to the Eskimos of today. We must, however, keep these first seal hunters in perspective, for by comparison even with those who immediately followed them in the cultural sequence, these people of the Denbigh Flint Complex of about 5,000 years ago were themselves exceedingly primitive.

There were other cultures developing almost simultaneously in Alaska: one about 450 kilometres (280 miles) to the north known as the Old Whaling Culture which,

when influenced by the Denbigh people advanced from hunting seals to the hunting of smaller species of whale; another in the Aleutian Islands that by about 2000 BC was way ahead in their hunting techniques and better equipped than any other culture to come on the scene during the next 2,000 years. Besides their impressive inventory of pronged harpoons and fishing spears, bird darts, fish-hooks, bolas and knives, and their stone "blubber lamps" with which they provided light and heat, it is even thought likely they had skin-covered boats— the larger *umiak* which could take up to a ton in weight, and that fast, sleek craft, the *kayak*. True, these Aleuts were not of the same ethnic group as the Eskimos further north, but since it is pretty certain that they had come on to the islands from the mainland of Alaska, the comparison to me seems relevant.

By about 2000 BC, as we have seen, Proto-Eskimos had appeared at several locations along the arctic coast of both Canada and north-

It is often assumed that the prehistorian's only clues as to what sort of clothing the Eskimos wore and what sort of life they led are to be found in the few crude artefacts he is able to dig up. But in fact a great deal of detail can be added to the picture from a study of the folklore and social character of the people as a whole.

13

Fig. 3: it is now generally believed that the last migration to cross the Bering "bridge" arrived in what is now called Alaska sometime between 15,000 and 10,000 years ago, and that these Arctic Mongoloids were the ancestors of the Eskimos. Archaeological evidence, however, suggests that it was not until about 3000 BC that these hunters finally adapted to life on the coast and started to spread out in search of new hunting territory.

Over the next 3,000 years as the race struggled for survival, some groups, such as the Sarqaq, became caught in a cultural trap—a backwater in which they stagnated and eventually died out while others, notably the Bering Sea and Alaskan tribes, through the stimulus of nearby cultures developed and refined their hunting techniques and finally gave birth in about AD 900 to that phenomenon which is known as the Thule.

Within one generation, two at the most, the first wave of this new culture had swept right across the Arctic and by 1300 there was not a single tribe that had escaped being crushed or influenced by it.

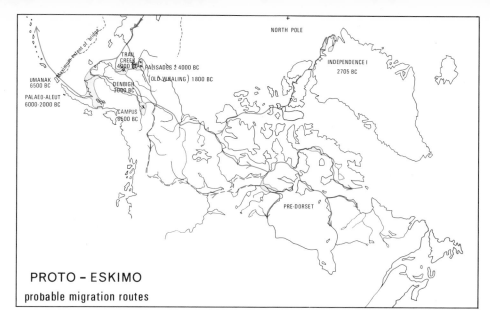

PROTO – ESKIMO
probable migration routes

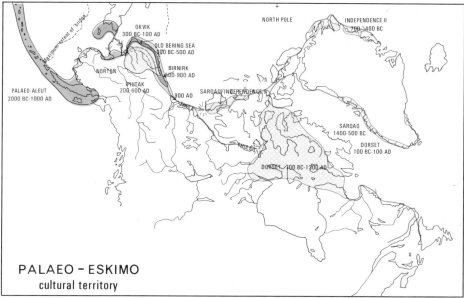

PALAEO – ESKIMO
cultural territory

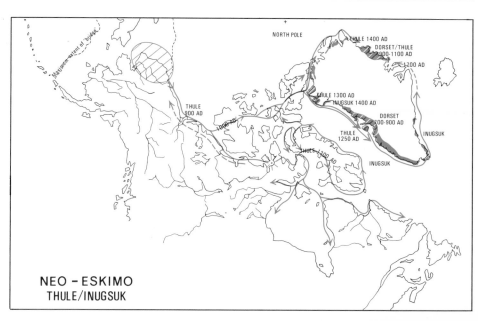

NEO – ESKIMO
THULE/INUGSUK

east Greenland. In Canada this stage in Eskimo development is called the Pre-Dorset culture. It lasted approximately from 4,000 to 2,800 years ago, whereas in Greenland the first wave of immigrants known as Independence 1 arrived about 4,680 years ago and were followed by a second group about 1,500 years later. Both the Pre-Dorset people and the Greenland infiltrations were clearly oriented towards life at the coast, but in terms of their cultural development, their artefacts seem to indicate that they had advanced very little on the Denbigh culture in spite of the distance these people had covered and the great variety of conditions they must have encountered.

Neither group seem to have made use of the blubber lamp, but then, it is known that the climate was milder than it is now. The Arctic Ocean was less choked with pack ice and the coasts (particularly in North Greenland) were littered with driftwood which had been carried by the currents across the ocean from Siberia. The bones and dung of muskoxen were also a source of fuel for the people who reached Greenland—indeed, so plentiful were the muskoxen in those days, it is hardly surprising that the Independence people did not develop their latent talent for hunting the sea mammals. Nor is there any indication that they had dogs. The bones of dogs have been found at several Pre-Dorset sites, and in Alaska at the site of the Old Whaling culture in Kotsebue Sound (450 kilometres [280 miles] north of Norton Sound) which dates from about the same period; but here, once again, we are back in what appears to be the breeding ground of all new cultural developments and at the start of a new phase.

No attempt to summarize the dying phase, however, would be complete without mentioning the Caribou Eskimos. On the face of

It is of course not surprising that they left so few clues behind them. On their migrations and at their summer camps (as at this one near Angmagssalik on the east coast of Greenland in 1906)`they used skin-covered tents for shelter and skin-covered boats to transport their gear from one location to another. Even the rings of stones which had been used to hold down their tents are sometimes difficult to spot 2,000 or 3,000 years later.

what little evidence we have to date, it would seem that throughout the entire circumpolar North there was, in prehistoric times, one basic culture from which individual groups gradually broke away—some adapting to the forests, others to the sea coasts, leaving behind on the tundra of the interior a few isolated groups of an originally vigorous and healthy people. In a sense the Caribou people became the living fossils from a stage in the development of the Eskimo long since washed away

in the classification of cultures, for this so-called Choris culture was no more than a village of degenerates who survived less than 300 years.

They were followed, or possibly ousted, by a tribe from Norton Sound who, it is believed, were the linguistic ancestors of all modern Eskimos. They were skilful seal hunters who had adopted many of the techniques of the Palaeo-Aleuts on the Aleutian Islands; an artistic people who had learnt how to make

The skin-covered boat had been in existence long before the Eskimos had ventured out in their own crude version 4,000 years ago. But the key to their success as hunters, and indeed to their very survival as a race, lay not so much in the design of the umiak, but in the use to which it was put. From this frail craft they hunted whales and with the perfection of this technique, the Thule culture had set out from Alaska to conquer the rest of the Arctic.

by the fast flow of time—a culture trapped in a backwater into which inadvertently it had drifted many thousands of years before. Perhaps the key to any understanding of the Proto-Eskimo lies in the study, not of artefacts 4,000 to 5,000 years old, but rather of those few, impoverished people who survived right through to quite recent times.

The Palaeo-Eskimo

What happened to the Old Whaling culture we do not know, for the Choris culture which appeared at the same location about 2,700 years ago, in many respects seems to bear a closer resemblance to the more "primitive" Denbigh Flint Complex. It is as though a cultural hiccup momentarily had checked the slow but continuous flow of information and experience from one generation to the next. But it serves to illustrate a common error

and decorate ceramics. The influence of this Norton culture in Alaska, however, was soon overtaken by a contemporary culture based on St Lawrence Island at the southern entrance of the Bering Strait, and another which appeared about the second century AD on the north-west coast. But these two, the Okvik and Ipiutak, were really too far advanced to be classed as Palaeo-Eskimo, and to find any other cultures in this category we must move eastwards through Canada to Greenland where we come across the Sarqaq culture which dates back to 3,400 years ago and lasted for almost a thousand years.

The origin of the Sarqaq culture is obscure. There are certain similarities with Independence 1 of north-east Greenland, and yet the Sarqaq people crossed Smith Sound from Canada about 400 years later. It is possible that they may have started out as a Pre-Dorset migra-

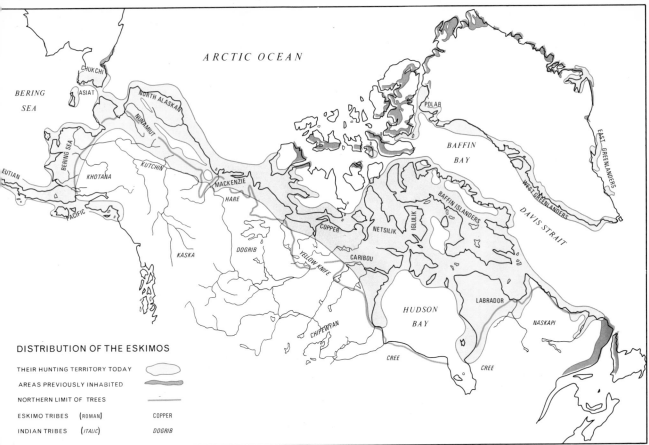

DISTRIBUTION OF THE ESKIMOS

THEIR HUNTING TERRITORY TODAY	
AREAS PREVIOUSLY INHABITED	
NORTHERN LIMIT OF TREES	
ESKIMO TRIBES (ROMAN)	COPPER
INDIAN TRIBES (ITALIC)	DOGRIB

tion and changed along the way. It is equally possible that they were, like the Independence people, an isolated tribe of hunters who had taken the more northerly route through arctic Canada and come in contact with no other tribes over a period of several generations. Once across Smith Sound and on Greenland soil, however, they are easier to trace, and from the many sites along the west and south-east coasts it would seem, initially at least, that they were fairly primitive.

But we should not classify these people with the Proto-Eskimos simply on account of this. The Sarqaq hunters were the first human beings to move down the west coast of Greenland. It was in a sense a dead end—a cultural backwater not unlike the one in which the Caribou Eskimos had become trapped, and like them, the Sarqaq people would have remained primitive right through to their inevitable extinc-

tion had not the Greenland ice cap occupied so much space that they were obliged to adapt to life at the coast. At the same time, we should be careful not to overrate them, for the climate during the time the Sarqaq people were on the coast of Greenland was comparatively warm and dry, and it is significant that with the slight deterioration in the climate that occurred about 2,500 years ago, they died out.

For the next 400 years, no human voice was heard along the whole 40,200-kilometre (25,000-mile) coastline of this the largest island in the world, and when voices of men were heard again, they were men of a different culture. But like the Sarqaq people, the origin of the Dorset culture is uncertain. Some prehistorians believe that these people were of Indian origin, for as one of them graphically puts it: "their artefacts smell of the forest". Others are of the opinion that they

There are about 40,000 Eskimos in Alaska, 18,000 in the Canadian Arctic and 50,000 in Greenland —a total of 108,000. It is, however, extremely difficult to obtain reliable figures, and the area of their territory is also hard to calculate. Although in theory the entire arctic region north of the treeline is their homeland, over 2 million square kilometres is covered by glacial ice and a great deal of the ice-free land is uninhabited. But at certain times of the year their hunting territory includes large areas of frozen sea.

17

were the descendants of those early arctic-Mongoloid hunters who had come in contact with Indians. But whatever their origin, they were clearly a remarkable people, for even as early as 4,000 years ago (in the Pre-Dorset stage of their development) there appear certain elements that foreshadow the Thule culture which did not flood into the Dorset area until about 700 years ago.

Their territory was vast. Even by keeping strictly to what has so far been proved it appears to have extended from Newfoundland in the south, up through the Hudson Bay region into the arctic archipelago, and across from there to Greenland where they occupied the whole of the west and south-east coasts. We know too that they went after every type of animal that moved across land and every sea mammal except the whale. But it would seem that they directed their skill and ingenuity only towards hunting, for their winter dens were nothing better than four sod walls and a ceiling of skin.

They knew about soapstone and from this material carved blubber lamps, bowls and cooking-pots, but "art" for its own sake or even in its more practical form as a design for better living does not seem to have occurred to them until about the year AD 500 when sculpture and decorative art spread across the whole Dorset area with an almost explosive force. They had by that time reached the peak of their cultural development beyond which they had neither the vision nor the desire to go. They had sledges, but had no dogs. They had the *kayak*, but not the skill to hunt from it. They had all the equipment for a way of life adapted to the sea, but without exception, every piece was crude.

It was traces of this Dorset culture that Eric the Red's Green-land settlers found in AD 986, but the people themselves had gone. It was this same culture in Canada which was driven out of its old hunting territory along the arctic coast about AD 1300 when the flood gates were opened in Alaska to release the culture that was to crush or swallow up every tribe or village that happened to be in the path of its relentless advance eastwards across the Arctic. But to see how this phenomenon which is called the Thule culture had evolved, we must return yet again to the Bering Strait region and step back in time one millennium.

The Thule phenomenon

Whether it was a mutation of genes or merely a caprice of nature which triggered off the evolution of that culture which is known as Thule is anybody's guess. The people of the Denbigh Flint Complex were not truly Eskimo, nor were the Sarqaq or the Dorset people, and the Okvik—almost, but not quite. Since, however, we need search no further than the latter for a way through to the Thule culture, let us take a closer look at the Okvik people, who appeared as if from nowhere over 2,000 years ago.

It is immediately evident from their technology that this culture was far in advance of the rest. Where then did they come from? One unlikely hypothesis suggests their ancestors were left stranded on St Lawrence Island when the Bering "bridge" flooded, and there, in isolation, they managed not only to survive 8,000 years of inbreeding, but to confound the science of genetics by developing an intellect sharper and more inventive than any other tribe within a radius of 3,200 kilometres (2,000 miles)—and twice that distance across territories occupied by people of their own ethnic group.

And the other possibilities? Either they were an Alaskan phenomenon which spread from the south-west, and crossed the Bering Strait to the Asiatic side where the culture took root and rapidly developed; or they were a late immigration from the Siberian mainland. Either way—their appearance in the Bering Strait region dramatically accelerated the progress of man towards his mastery of the arctic environment; in fact, on first looking at their equipment, it is hard to see any design which could be improved upon or even any vital omissions.

With the weapons they had they could harpoon, lance, shoot, spear or snare any creature that came within range. They had *umiaks* and *kayaks*, sledges and dogs, and time on their hands to tattoo themselves and complicate their lives with "gods" and magical rituals which they barely understood.

It was a development which, according to the archaeologists, passed through two more stages (the Old Bering Sea and the Birnirk) before reaching its maturity in the Thule; but the progression as I see it was more a change of character than a change in the material culture—a subtle change which came about through contact with neighbouring tribes, among them the Ipiutak who were essentially an inland culture, and impulses which had reached them from very much further afield—from Siberia or south-west Alaska. But we must remember here that we are dealing with a phenomenon, not simply another culture—a phenomenon which finally materialized about AD 900 in the region of Cape Parry in Amundsen Gulf and along the north and north-west coasts of Alaska. By this time the Birnirk had simply become Thule. By the eleventh century the Thules were ready to set out on their triumphal conquest of the entire arctic coast.

Within one generation, two at the most, the first wave of Thule hit the coast of north-west Greenland and spread out. By 1250 they had reached Disco Bay on the west coast, and by AD 1300, while the Thule hunters were crushing or driving out all the Dorset people from their coastal hunting grounds in the Canadian Arctic, new waves of Thule immigrants were flooding into Greenland via the ice bridge which for a few months of each year links Ellesmere Island to Greenland at Smith Sound.

Driftwood was plentiful along some stretches of the Arctic coast, but in other parts it was not, and the Eskimos in those regions were obliged to make the runners of their sledges from frozen fish and rolled-up frozen caribou skins. In the picture, the parcel of fish is being trodden into shape before putting on a coating of moss and slush and, finally, a few coats of clear water which will turn instantly to ice.

19

All this time they had been learning, adapting, developing. They were big-game hunters—brave, skilful, aggressive people. With courage enough to tackle even the enormous baleen whale, the small parties of Norsemen they came across on the west coast of Greenland would certainly have been no match for them; but there is no evidence that, in the early stages at least, these contacts were anything other than peaceful and curious encounters in which these two very different people weighed each other up.

The very practical Eskimos immediately absorbed every idea that could be adapted to their way of life. The Norsemen, on the other hand, being in their own estimation the superior of the two cultures, learnt nothing whatsoever from these "swarthy, evil-looking men", and in consequence, the balance of survival swung against them. Their West Settlement (in the present district of Godthab) which had been established by some of Eric the Red's colonists between AD 986 and the turn of the century, and which at one time had been a flourishing community of some ninety farms, by 1345 was deserted. No trace could be found of any human being dead or alive, Christian or heathen —only a few horses, goats, cows and sheep, and they, without the company of men, had all returned to the wild.

What happened to the Norsemen is a mystery. But this much we know for certain: with the extinction of the West Settlement, the bell had tolled also for those in the larger colony to the south, and for the next hundred years the people there had lived in fear that their lifelines with Norway would one day be broken; that their crops would fail, their livestock die and that they themselves would succumb to the damp and penetrating cold. And with all but the last of these fears fulfilled they had bowed their heads to the castigations of their God, and by the time the Eskimos like vultures moved in, the cries of the victims were too weak to be heard.

These Eskimos, however, were not of the Thule culture. With what had been learnt or taken from the Norsemen, the Thule people had become a better-equipped, more vigorous and expansive culture, and with this change of character had come a change of name. To some extent, there was also a change of environment, for the Inugsuk, as this new culture was called, had taken a liking to the west coast of Greenland and abandoned their old hunting territory to the north of Melville Bay to any late immigrants who might be skilful enough to hunt it. And that rich game territory did not remain free from the human predator for long. Migrations of Thule hunters in waves kept coming across Smith Sound from Canada right up to the eighteenth century. But these waves usually were small (three or four family groups at a time) and very few of these Thule hunters moved far enough down the west coast to come in contact with the Inugsuk people who, even by the fifteenth century, were losing some of their whaling skills, and replacing this loss by perfecting other skills which in a sense forged the last link in the complete adaptation of the hunter to the sea.

In a design of *kayak* sleeker and faster than anything man had made before, these hunters, accompanying their *umiaks* in flotillas, cut through the sunless channel which today is called Prince Christian Sound to *nunap tunua*—"the rear of the country"—and on, up the stark and ice-choked south-east coast of Greenland. At about the

same time, small parties of hunters migrating around the north coast from the Thule District were closing the gap, and by the sixteenth century we may assume there was not one stretch of the entire Greenland coastline which had not been seen by the Eskimos from their *kayaks* or from their sledges.

But prehistory is not made up simply of cold archaeological "facts", nor does it come abruptly to an end when the written record, subjective though it is, takes over from the guess. There are other clues to the nature of man concealed in his legends and myths—clues which we cannot afford to overlook if we are to discover what motivated the Eskimo.

The coast near Jakobshavn.

CHAPTER TWO

THE VOICE FROM
THE PAST

Eskimo mythology was made up of the first profound thoughts of primitive man—his first attempt to relate himself to what he could see about him and to that other more malevolent world that was inhabited by spirits.

But as a tale spun in the dawn of time and handed down by word of mouth through countless generations of men, is it not reasonable to suppose that the myth may have drifted from the original story in the course of those many thousands of years during which it has been recited? Among the Eskimos, if a story-teller deviates by as much as a word from the traditional tale he is ridiculed and this he cannot bear. How else are we to account for the many versions of the same theme which are to be found throughout the Arctic? Some anthropologists believe that the oral tradition of the Eskimos broke down during their migrations, and that the more isolated tribes had no alternative but to think afresh. If this is so it presupposes that all primitive people, when faced with the same situations in life, the same phenomena of nature and the same sense of impotence in the face of the overwhelming power of the supernatural, will ask themselves the same questions and answer them in much the same way and although I do not entirely agree, there is some

evidence to support this theory.

Take the creation for example: of the many races of people whose philosophy was based on the concept that function followed logically from function, few had even the vaguest idea of an initiator, or creator of that sequence of functions. Certainly, in the Eskimo myths of Creation, there are no concepts which come anywhere near to the sophistication of those which form the basis of the Hebrew religion or the mythology of ancient Egypt which was in its infancy at about the same time that the Eskimos were spreading out across the Arctic.

The fact is, the Eskimos, like so many other primitive peoples, were too preoccupied with their daily struggle for survival to give much thought to the mystery of their origin or to what sort of "life" followed death. Their myths reflect this— especially those of the eastern arctic which, although colourful enough when dealing with the phenomena that affected their health and their skill at the hunt are much less striking and inventive when explaining mysteries which to them were of little consequence.

In the beginning [they say] there was nothing but water. Then suddenly, one day, it began to rain rocks—and that is how land was created. The people, they came out of mounds of earth, but at that time they were only babies they could not see, they could

The Eskimo concept of the source of all power is beautiful but vague. In a sense it is "the world out there" and that feeling of awe which he experiences in its company.

not even crawl—they just lay there sprawling and feeding themselves with handfuls of mud until at last a woman came looking for them. She had made some babies' clothes in the hope that one day she would find some babies to care for, so she was very happy when she found them and after dressing the babies, she took them all home—and that is how there came to be so many people in the world.

Where the woman came from the myth doesn't say; but the Eskimos rarely question the stories they are told, nor does it seem to puzzle them if one part of the story is quite clearly seen to contradict another for, to put in in their own words: "who is so wise that he can prove wrong something he does not understand."

There are of course variations on the Creation myth even in the eastern Arctic.

In the beginning [so another story goes] the world was inhabited by only two men, both of whom were great magicians. They were, however, not so great that they could create children, and this made them very sad for having grown tired of each other's company they wanted to increase their number. But one day, the cleverer of the two magicians had a bright idea which was to make them both very happy: he transformed himself into a woman, and by this new arrangement, became the mother of mankind.

Needless to say, there is as much mystery over where the two magicians came from as there is over the origin of the foster mother in the previous tale.

All because of Raven

Move westwards towards Alaska and, as one would expect, the stories are richer and more complex, for Greenland after all was the end of the line and as far from the influence of the Asiatic and Indian cultures as it is possible to get. This is not to say that the folklore of the North Alaskan Eskimos is lacking in character and originality—they borrowed the Raven myth from the Indians but credited him in their own myths with no less a feat than creating the world and releasing daylight. The myth becomes "all-Eskimo" in character, however, not through the acts of Raven, but through the self-contradictions which are so typical of all Eskimo myths and the casual omission of any logical progress or plot.

In the beginning, when the world was in darkness, the only land in the world was a patch of ground no bigger than a house—and in that house lived a woman and an old man who was her father. One day the woman went out to collect some snow for the melting pot. As she was bending down scraping the snow into her pot she saw a feather floating towards her on the sea and when she opened her mouth, it floated in and she swallowed it. From that moment the woman was pregnant, and the baby she had as a result of this, had a raven's bill instead of a mouth. Now one day, when the woman was trying to amuse her child, he pointed to a round bladder that was hanging on the wall above the old man's bed, for he wanted to play with it. "No, you can't have it" the woman said firmly, and the child began to cry. At last she could stand his crying no longer and gave him the bladder; but in playing with it, he broke it and light flooded out. Soon light was spreading out all over the world, and when the old man saw it, he rushed into the house and snatched the bladder from the child before all the daylight was released so that there would be both day and night, and not just daylight all the time.

And again, it is told, now that there was light, Raven wanted to go in search of a land far away which the old man believed existed, but which he assumed was impossible to reach. "No, you must not go" the old man warned, "it's dangerous out there." But the boy begged and begged until the old man agreed to let him go. They say that Raven paddled the old man's kayak for a long time before he finally came to a place where he saw land bobbing up and down in the water as though it was a whale, and that when Raven saw this he was afraid. After a while, however, his courage returned, and he harpooned the land as it rose out of the sea and held it fast by the harpoon line until it moved no more. And when the land was fixed in place, Raven got out of the kayak and as he walked about on the island, the sea began to move away until there was no sea in sight. And so it is because of Raven that people ever since that time have been able to live in the world.

Legends in the eastern Arctic say the first people were much stronger than they are now and that every man was a magician. When they

wanted to move to another place they simply sat in their houses and commanded them to fly, and houses might still have been able to fly today had not one magician complained about the noise the other magicians' houses made when they were flying through the air. They say that all the houses in the world heard his words for his voice was more powerful than his neighbours', and that it is because the houses were ashamed that they have remained stationary ever since.

They also say that in those days snow could burn and that fire sometimes fell from the sky. They say too that at first, people did not know how to die and in a while became so numerous that they overpopulated the Earth. Then there came a mighty flood which swept most of them away. Traces of that flood they say can be found even today on the tops of the high hills where there are shells.

It may be that the flood of which they speak in the legends refers to the flooding of their old hunting grounds north of the Bering Strait

Exactly when the first kayak was made is impossible to say. It is, however, fairly certain that it was being used in the Aleutian Islands at least 4,000 years ago. And the fact that it features in the Raven myth clearly indicates that the Eskimos regard it as a craft of great antiquity.

in the area now known as the Chukchi Sea, but that flooding was not as cataclysmic as the legends seem to imply—it was in fact, as we have already seen, a very gradual rise in the level of the world ocean spanning several hundreds of years. So what value, if any, have these legends and myths if at best they are no nearer to the truth than this? But ask this and you must first define truth. An opinion which is different to the rest is no less likely to be correct because it does not conform ". . . some men hear a different drummer and march a different pace." Is not truth then, no more certain than one man's interpretation of it? This may be so in the case of the sophisticated mind; but it is not so in the case of the primitive.

To the Eskimo, truth is more in the nature of a blind faith in the words of the old folk, "for there are no lies with age", and no man can measure his wisdom with the fathers of his tribe. They *believed* their folk-lore, and even if we allow for some distortion in the original stories, we are bound to marvel at the freshness and pure childlike innocence these stories still possess in spite of the many millions of mouths that have recited them, and from the ideas they express, draw certain conclusions about the men who first spun those myths.

The world of the spirits

We can take it that the early Eskimos, in common with all other primitive peoples, looked upon their daily life as a variety of functions, and that it was as a limitless number of vaguely defined functions that they saw their surrounding world. We can also quite safely assume that in the earliest stages of their development they had no "religious" feelings; but rather, an instinctive acceptance of a spiritual world born of fear and the primitive concept that everything that could be seen or sensed possessed the power to influence. Among this great variety of "powers" however, very few were personified and none regarded as gods. Nor did these powers form a coherent whole or gang together in groups—each was mutually independent and no one power could thwart another. Nevertheless, they crowded in on the Eskimos and greatly complicated his way of life (which was already quite hard enough) for these powers that were inherent in everything were all too easily offended and much less easily appeased.

According to some of the early missionaries, the Eskimos had brought these problems upon themselves, for the *inua*, as they called each thing's spirit or living "owner", was in a sense the projection of their own pagan fears and doubts into

Communal dwellings at Angmagssalik, East Greenland, c. 1900. It was in their dens (especially during the long polar nights) that the folklore of their race was handed down from one generation to the next.

every creature, object and phenomenon of nature—in much the same way that a child instinctively credits things with a vitality that is human, and the ability to think and feel, and sometimes even speak.

But the Eskimos were not simply living in a state of fearful co-existence with the world of the spirits—at some stage in their cultural development they had further complicated their existence by the discovery that a man had a soul and that his soul was vulnerable. This "soul" was called *târneq*, which means "something like darkness" or "something like a shadow". It was a vague concept which, as it spread across the Arctic, took on many different forms. Usually it looked like the body of the person or animal it inhabited, but on a very much smaller scale. Among the West Greenland tribes it was generally believed that if the soul was stolen, the body would fall sick and die unless it was quickly retrieved by an Eskimo magician.

The name itself was a sort of soul —it stayed near the body when it died, not leaving it until it was called upon to enter the body of a new-born child. Some Eskimos believed that the child would thus inherit many of the qualities of its namesake (which did not necessarily have to be of the same sex). Some believed that the child was the reincarnation of the one that had died, but as we shall see later, their idea of reincarnation was somewhat different to the Western concept— less so with animals: any animal could be reborn providing the taboos were correctly observed; indeed, these taboos *had* to be observed, for unless all animals that were killed or about to be killed were treated with the utmost respect, they would revenge themselves upon the man who had killed them. Small wonder then that the Eskimos, whose food

Witchcraft, once the prerogative of every adult Eskimo, has finally died out and the tupilak, *which for almost 5,000 years was an instrument of evil, has become a lucrative sideline for the Eskimos.*

Strictly speaking these miniature ivory carvings merely depict the tupilak, *for the real tupilak was a monster made and magically brought to life by an Eskimo who wanted to rid himself of an enemy. The tupilak was put together in some lonely place and sent out to attack in whatever form it had been made to represent; as a seal or a walrus it would capsize the victim when he was in his* kayak; *as a bear it would tear him apart. But since* tupilaks *had no sense of loyalty and lacked an independent will, they could be turned by an Eskimo magician against the man or woman who had created them.*

There was, and of course will always be, a very special bond between the young ones and the old. For the old were wise, the old were kind, but above all, the old had time on their hands to feed the daydreams of the young and a lifetime's experience on which to draw when answering the questions of the children in their care.

consisted entirely of "souls", produced not a single man who dared to indulge his doubt, much less openly challenge the accepted beliefs of his race.

There was a third factor in the Eskimo philosophy—one which concerned itself with the greater mystery—the "master" of all power. This concept they called *sila*. It was a force neither for good nor evil— an impersonal force as invisible as air. And this in a sense is what it was. Where it came from, the Eskimos did not know, nor did they ever venture a guess. They simply accepted it as *Pínga*—"something up there"— something to be feared; something of which they were in awe.

Less remote than *sila* or *silap inua* as it was sometimes called, was a force almost as great, and even more greatly feared. This they called *ímap inua*, and its shape and genesis was known right across the Arctic by every Eskimo who came in contact with the sea, for this power, in the shape of an old crone, ruled over all creatures that lived in the sea and held sway over all storms, fogs, rain and sleet. In the West Greenland version of the myth,

Sedna, or *Arnaquagssâq* as she is called in Greenland, when she was a young orphan girl, had been pushed over the side of a boat by her guardian who wanted to get rid of her. It is said she clung to the side of the boat and that the man had to cut off her fingers before she would release her grip, and as she sank to the bottom of the sea, he threw overboard her dog and her lamp. Ever since that time she has lived on the sea bed all alone, her long hair matted thick with vermin because she had no fingers with which to grip a comb. And they say that the sea creatures would hide in her hair whenever a taboo had been broken and would not be released unless, of his own accord, the offender confessed, or an *angákoq* had swum down to the bottom of the sea to comb the animals out of her hair and appease her anger towards the hunters who depended on her for food and clothing and the blubber for their lamps.

In this story, man is starving because the seals have stayed away, and there can be only one explanation for this—*Arnaquagssâq* is angry, and she is only ever made angry when a taboo is broken. And so the thought has traced a circle and returned to its point of departure: man is starving because of man's foolishness. But this story is not typical of the Eskimo myth—in fact, it is the only example I have ever come across which seems remotely to have been influenced by the logic of cause and effect—and this is surprising. Since the Eskimos could hardly have coexisted with the spirit world without constantly being reminded through illness, bad weather, starvation, and countless other setbacks of the consequences of breaking the rules, one would have expected all their myths to peddle a moral or take the form of a parable as do the myths and legends of so many other races of people. And so we have the first hint that the Eskimos were different—a race that worshipped no gods; a race without chiefs; a race that bent all the rules except the law of nature by which as predators they were bound.

Food for thought

Like all predators they regarded hard times as a thing of the past, for the present by comparison never seemed as bad, and the future, according to their philosophy, simply did not exist. Seen from this point of view, the more gruesome the story, the more effective was the balm. But let me give you two examples translated as closely as possible from the stories as they were told to me a few years ago by Amaunalik from the Thule District —a remarkable old woman who used no gestures or facial contortions to dramatize her tales; only her voice—that soft, expressive, almost magical voice that intoned all stories at the same slow pace, as though each word was feeding on the atmosphere the sound itself created.

One of our forefathers, [she would begin, clearing her throat with the customary show of embarrassment at having attracted an audience] one of our forefathers, it is told, he used to go out waiting at a seal's breathing hole now and again when he was starving. He, having gone out hunting one day, his wife (fearing that he would eat her when he returned) her sealskin jacket she stuffed it with grass. And when she had stuffed it, she laid it in her sleeping place, and in the igloo passage, it is told, she made a cave. Later, when she had hidden herself in the cave, her husband came home, and thinking it was his wife lying in her sleeping place, he stabbed her. But he discovered when he had stabbed it, the sealskin jacket was quite without a human being, and when he saw this he began to boil water. And when it was boiling, it is told, his thigh he began to cook it. Then— part of himself he having put to the boil—he cried out because he was dying, while in the pot his thigh was boiling!

"*Ajor!*—what a pity!" Amaunalik would exclaim at the end of each gruesome story, and then, looking around at her audience, burst out laughing as though the very indignity of the mutilated man had suddenly become ridiculous. Soon they were all roaring with laughter and with tears pumping from their eyes and their bodies heaving they would eventually slump into a silence broken only now and then by a shuddered sigh. Only then, as the horror of the story crept into their bones and began to work its healing miracles upon the fear within their souls would Amaunalik clear her throat and start another tale more horrible than the last.

And when they began to starve, it is told, Igi'marsus'suak his dwelling place companions he began to eat them, and his children also. Arnaqa his wife, it is told, she used to boil them after first having gathered fuel of willow branches, and the heads before he ate them, Arnaqa she deloused them. At last, it is told, Arnaqa's younger brother him alone he had left and also wanting to eating him, Igi'marsus'suak he killed him. Gathering fuel of willow branches, Arnaqa her younger brother she began to cut up and while delousing his head and crying bitterly it is told Igi'marsus'suak to his wife in anger said: "Boiling him and weeping over him!" Arnaqa thus replied: "Indeed no, with blowing fire my eyes they only water—I cry not" she said to her husband, lying. He then ate him up, and again it is told, he intended also to eat his wife and sent her out to gather willow branches, but fleeing she went away, her husband entirely leaving!

Amaunalik had been weaned as a child on stories such as these. Some she liked, others she liked less; but none had she the right as an Eskimo to reject, for the folklore of her people was their only link with the past beyond the living memory of the old folk of the tribe.

Fact or fantasy

From their legends they learned about the *Tunit*—a race of giants who hunted on foot with only a

When he sang for his own amusement or to entertain his friends, the Eskimo's songs were invariably statements of his love of life or a mild lampoon at the expense of one of his listeners. His magic songs were something else. These he regarded as property and never sang out loud in the presence of other men.

spear and a knife. They say in winter when the *Tunit* hunted at a seal's breathing hole in the ice, they would light a blubber lamp and lean over it so that their long seal-skin coat would form a "tent" in which the heat was confined. Inside this coat the giants they say were as naked as the day they were born, and you could always tell which of them had fallen asleep while waiting for a seal to appear by the burn marks on their bellies. They say too that these giants could outrun a caribou and haul a walrus out of the sea as though it were a seal. But, in spite of their formidable strength, these giants were driven out of their territory by the forefathers of the Eskimos who live in that territory today. Perhaps we can assume from this that the *Tunit* of the legends were those people of the Dorset culture who were overrun by the Thule tribes about AD 1300.

Also among their legends are many which tell of the *Kavdlunait*, a people foreign to the Arctic—a fair-skinned people who in some respects were cleverer than the *inuit* or "real men" as they called

themselves—a people, nevertheless, who even from the earliest encounters were clearly not to be trusted. In fairness to the Norsemen, they regarded the Eskimos—or "Skraelings" as they called them—with even greater suspicion, so it is hardly surprising that from an atmosphere as perfidious as this should come stories mostly of bloodshed and revenge. But rarely do the legends say what triggered off these feuds.

In Aron of Kangeq's story of the promiscuous Navaranaq, however, we are left in little doubt. Having grown tired of the attentions of the men at her own camp, she had taken to visiting the Norsemen at a nearby farm, which of course rankled with the Eskimo hunters and boiled the blood of the farmers' wives. Her vanity alas was not satisfied with this, and she set about provoking the Eskimos and Norsemen to fight each other for her attentions—which they did, and the Eskimos won. In the legend it is said "the hunters then turned on the harlot, tied thongs to her hair and arms and dragged her at full speed across the

The folklore of the Eskimo, rich and vital though it was, found no visual medium of expression except through sculpture — at least, not until Aron of Kangeq turned to the medium of painting in the 1850s. Through it he found a way of illustrating scenes from his vast repetoire of stories, four of which (including the one of the Eskimos revenging themselves on Navaranaq) are shown here.

rocks and jagged ice along the coast, and when her back was torn to shreds they asked her—'are you having fun, Navaranaq?', to which she replied, 'Indeed I am!' So they dragged her over and over the course until the entrails were pouring out of her back, and when they saw this they asked her once more, 'are you having fun, Navaranaq?', but to this second question, according to the legend, Navaranaq gave no answer.''

Even in the Eskimo tales which relate to historical events such as the attacks on the Norse settlements by the Basque whalers about the middle of the fifteenth century, or events as recent as the last migration from Canada to Greenland where the legends are only 100 years old, it is impossible to tell where the facts end and the fantasy begins. But what use had the Eskimos for a more precise history or for a more rational explanation of the mysteries of the world than those spun in the dawn of time. The old stories made no demands upon their intellect. They were simply a form of entertainment —a pleasant way of wiling away the hours or days that they spent waiting for the weather to change, or for the winter to draw to a close.

True, their stories were grotesque and their sense of humour even in its mildest form thoroughly obscene, but only by "civilized" standards, and what right have the civilized to judge—at least the Eskimos did not spawn hypocrites, bigots and freaks. They laughed at themselves and at their fellow men. They laughed at sex and its organs, at all natural functions of the human body and at any pretence at dignity which placed a man on a higher plane than the animals he hunted, while the animals themselves remained sacrosanct and entered his stories, as they did his life, by the divine grace of providence.

And so through the centuries the tales droned on, tale after tale in endless procession, with the quick continuing where the dead had left off like a lifetime's experience that had stuck in a groove, for in the Eskimo language there was no word for "fiction" before the white invasion, nor was there such a thing as "licence" even in the telling of an ordinary tale. If a story could not be retold exactly as it had been heard, the narrator was bound by his personal honour to admit his version was inferior or, better still, keep silent.

Folklore and knowledge cannot spread if there is no physical route —no link between one culture and another. The "bridge" for instance between Canada and Greenland was nothing more than a skin of ice; but it is a route which is still used to this day by the hunters from the Thule District who cross Smith Sound to the Canadian side in search of polar bears.

CHAPTER THREE

THE FAMILY FORTRESS

The soft centre of any society is the individual. He is weak; he is vulnerable, and he protects himself in the only way he is able—by shrinking into the crowd. The crowd itself may be no more than a party of hunters—two or three families at the most; a group with no sense of identity with anyone outside their own small circle of kin. It may be a larger territorial group; one made up of many small but widely dispersed camps, all leaderless, but each bound by their allegiance to the clan. It may be a more complex and patriotically oriented group which is subdivided into smaller task groups coordinated by some form of bureaucratic administration or, at the far extreme of the nomadic and self-sufficient band of tribesmen, the monolothic State which commands loyalty to a political ideology regardless of creed, trade or colour of skin. But the more complex the organization, the more insecure a man becomes, for by the very nature of the civilized state, the goals he pursues in one group invariably conflict with those he pursues in another.

Of course, many of us know only one system—the one into which we were born. To swear by it we are told is our patriotic duty, and yet we do not have to dig too deeply into history to see the mistake of thinking that what worked for us will work also for the rest of the world, or to find in the colonial administrators' attitude towards the aboriginal, a more benign version of the same naïve assumption. The Eskimo society, for example, functioned at the lowest possible level of organization. Call it "primitive" if you like, but the fact is, their way of life was geared to simplicity, and any change in their system was bound, initially at least, to do more harm than good.

At the root of his existence was an instinct as basic as that of any animal he hunted; the instinct of self-preservation—the instinct to mate. Love was no prerequisite; neither was marriage the genuflection to morality that we of the more advanced civilizations have been conditioned to accept as the only foundation upon which a family can be built. It was simply a practical arrangement by which a man and a woman, both restricted by taboos from doing any job regarded as the prerogative of the opposite sex, joined forces in order to survive.

But this union, which we will call "marriage" in spite of the different connotation invested in that word by the Christian world, served another vital purpose—it extended the sphere of kinship. The couple had thus in one move become a viable economic unit which was capable, in theory at least, of sustaining and multiplying itself, and

Stone and turf dens are things of the past. But as long as they contain memories they will, by the old folk, still be preferred to the frame huts which have replaced them.

If there were more women than men and the hunting territory could support them, the hunters were polygamous. If there were more men than women then the society became polyandrous for the Eskimo was a practical man and his wife a practical woman.

Top: a Netsilik woman with her two husbands.

Right: Egaluk from Adelaide Peninsula with his two wives.

at the same time had become part of a mutually interdependent group— a family cooperative that would stick together through good times and bad, succour or come to the defence of their own blood kin and even seek vengeance on anyone who harmed any member of their clan.

Here then was the security that the individual lacked. Within this group he could move freely for his extended family was, so to speak, the inner keep of a fortress which protected him from any attack or adversity aimed at him by the outside world, while the outer walls of his fortress were made up of non-kin trading partners, pals, random sexual contacts and as many offspring as he had the time or the energy to produce.

Of course, put this way it sounds as though he was pretty well pro-tected, and so perhaps he would have been had he not been expected to accord to his kin the same protection they accorded him; but to see where the snag lay we must look a little more closely at the structure of the family and the tendency of the Eskimo to perpetuate feuds.

The inner circle

As we have already seen, the purpose of marriage was two-fold: to make one effective predator out of two essentially ineffective halves, and to extend the circle of kinship as far as it would stretch. The choice of partner, since there was rarely any complication of romantic love, was usually decided by the family, with the pros and cons of each candidate being carefully weighed to see which family "connection" would eco-

For as far back in time as the pre-historian is able to go, the communal bed has always been the only essential piece of furniture in an Eskimo family's home.

nomically be best. Marriage between cousins was considered undesirable, mainly on the grounds that such a union would not extend the kin ties into another family group, but apart from that there was always the fear that the offspring from such a union "were unlikely to be quite human". As for incestuous relationships between brothers and sisters —this was strictly taboo. In fact, the only case of such a relationship that I have ever come across is in the traditional myth of the Sun and Moon, both of whom, so it is told, lived here on Earth as sister and brother a long, long time ago.

They were young and carefree, so the story goes, and like all unmarried Eskimos, about as carnal as it is possible for a human being to be. Whenever there was any skittish fun or any cuddling going on, Sun and Moon were sure to be found right there in the thick of it for sexual games had become their adolescent passion. Even in that game they called "dousing the lights" —a game in which close kin were not, strictly speaking, supposed to join in—Sun and Moon could not resist putting themselves at risk.

They would wait until the lights were put out then break the rules and wriggle free and in the dark grope silently through the heavy press of sensual flesh in search for a partner with whom they would, without a word, make love, and not until after several months did Sun become suspicious that there was one man in that darkened room who against all the natural laws of chance was finding her too often.

But she kept her secret fear to herself and took a little soot from her lamp and when the same lover found her again she pressed her fingers against his cheek, and sure enough, when the lamps were re-lit, there was Moon with the mark of disgrace upon his face and Sun, on seeing this, blushed red and hot with shame. Then in her misery, it is said, she dipped a tuft of moss in blubber and setting it alight ran out of the house vowing for all the world to hear that she would run far away and never see her brother again.

order to play safe, they extended their taboos to cover every conceivable case: the adopted "child", for example, could not marry into its adopted family, nor could a man and woman born of different parents and at opposite ends of the Arctic get married if as children they had been adopted and brought up together as brother and sister under the same skin roof. It was a taboo for two brothers from one family to marry two sisters from another,

Moon is male and dangerous — throughout the Eskimo world this was believed to be so. But like all other powerful spirits or inue *he could be appeased if he was angry and, providing all the taboos associated with him were strictly observed, he could even be beneficient.*

But Moon chased after her and at that moment they were carried up into the sky where forever it is their fate to drift—the one with shame burning so hot that her light in summer warms the world; while the other on whose face in winter the smudge of soot can still be seen, shines with a much weaker light *pisoktut angut* as the Eskimos say: "because he is a man".

Of course, it *is* a myth, but we should not dismiss it simply on account of that, for even a story of pure fantasy must have a grain of truth. As for the Eskimos, they really believed that if by accident or intent they were to indulge in incest, the world they knew would come to an end. The Sun and Moon were their visible proof and their constant reminder on cloudless days of what might be their fate, and in

and for a widow to marry her dead husband's brother, his cousin, his father or even his father's bastard son. In fact, so many were there of these taboos that the only solution on some occasions was to migrate to another district to look for a suitable mate.

But even the long-range suitor might find he was courting trouble. For one thing, nowhere in the Arctic was there a surplus of women and the local men would almost certainly look upon a stranger as a poacher on their ground. Even a stranger who posed no threat was mistrusted and often beaten up then driven out of the territory—a pattern of behaviour identical to that found among packs of wolves and wild dogs. And even supposing the stranger was permitted to stay and found himself a wife, the chances are that she would be incompatible and very home-sick among her husband's family, for the way of life and the specialized skills of each hunting group varied greatly from place to place.

Lucky then was the man who, having sampled all the local girls in such games as "dousing the lights", discovered that his choice was as beautiful as she was passionate, as happy at work as she was at play and had family connections in almost every village in the district, for with such a girl as this for a wife he would be able to travel unmolested through any area where her kinfolk had influence. Luckier still was he if his choice had many brothers, all of whom were noted for their industry and skill, for by marrying into their circle of kin he would be entitled at any time to enlist their support and without embarrassment or fear of refusal could ask for food, shelter, clothing or comfort whenever he was in need.

But this, of course, is always supposing that her kin and his were agreeable to the marriage, and a suitable match as far as they were concerned had little or nothing to do with the compatibility of the principal pair. Much more important was whether the two families were of equal standing. Would, for example, the union of the two families be to their mutual advantage? Was there any bad feeling between them and, most important of all, was the other family involved in any blood feuds—for these revenge killings were like a contagious disease which passed from one family to another with the very act of coition that consummated marriage. Even families that were not involved in any blood feuds— families appalled by the futility of the whole concept of revenge by which a life was taken for a life were,

nevertheless, inexorably drawn into this self-destructive system by their obligation through marriage to support the spouse's kin.

It seems incredible that a society which in every other respect was responsible and compassionate and whose sole object it was to survive, should be unable to find a more sensible alternative to that murderous and masochistic game by which pawn took pawn until the smaller of the two feuding families

was completely annihilated. But is modern man any the wiser? He regards the blood feud as barbaric, but in the name of defence he marshals his armies and behind the smiling disguise of détente has devised ways and means of wiping his enemies off the face of the Earth in one great holocaust. So who then are we to disparage? Is not the killing of one Eskimo family by another compared with the wholesale destruction of a civilization no more than a difference of scale?

The extended family

It is evident from his myths and legends that the Eskimo was fully aware of the capricious nature of Fate, but whether in his stories he deliberately made use of irony as a means of expressing some perverse

The sun, being a woman, was not considered to be as powerful as the moon and in Eskimo mythology it plays only a minor role. Its return, nevertheless, was always welcomed after the long dark winter if only because it heralded the return of life.

Never are children denied affection or the freedom to express it.

twist of circumstances in a form that would entertain, we have no way of knowing. I suspect he was unaware, for example, of the irony of his own vulnerability. He had built for himself a fortress of protective kin and yet, should the life of any of his so-called protectors be taken in blood vengence for a killing, he was liable to be called upon to forfeit his own life in the cause of retribution. Had he ever stopped to ask himself what was the point, he would have grown in stature as a man but immediately become the target, for, among Eskimos, no one who asserts an opinion or has the temerity to make a stand against the accepted tradition survives long enough to change his mind. So his only course of action while there was still time and the stream of life flowed sweetly, was to extend his bonds of friendship into every camp and family in which some hapless relative of his might by accident at some future date plant the seeds of enmity. And in the Eskimo society, which if not perfect, at least was supple, he achieved this end through

It is often said that children are the same the world over, but this simply is not so for the laws of survival vary greatly from one society to the next. The competitive spirit which is regarded by our own aggressive society as an admirable quality, is anathema to the Eskimos whose very survival depends upon their compatibility.

voluntary associations, the most enjoyable of which were sexual.

It would, however, be quite wrong to think that sexual freedom among Eskimos was free-running and irresponsible. On the contrary, premarital sexual relations carried with them obligations which were binding not only on the principals concerned but also on their kin, and so seriously were these obligations taken that this "weakness" was sometimes used by men and women from the two feuding families as a means of bringing the bloodshed to an end; the argument being that the offspring from such illicit affairs were half-brothers or *qatanguutigiit* to their own children, and the relationship of formal cooperation that existed between them forbade any further hostility between their kin.

The term *qatanguutigiit* was used also for stepchildren, and for any offspring resulting from the habit of exchanging wives as a means of cementing the ties of friendship and cooperation between two trading partners. There was, of course, no stigma attached to illegitimacy nor was chastity seen by the Eskimos as a virtue. The sexual needs of the human being were by them regarded as perfectly natural, and any sexual relationship outside of marriage, providing it was "honourable", served to extend the individual's circle of friends into another family group which might at some future date be of some advantage not only to him but also to his kin.

If a boy, for example, while out travelling alone, came upon a village in which he had no relatives, he would immediately seek out the children of his father's trading partner and would be gladly received by them, for it would be assumed that, as with most trading partners, their fathers must at some time have exchanged their wives and that the possibility therefore existed that they were half-brothers to each other. Naturally it follows that for such a system to be of the maximum advantage to the children, their parents would not only have to recall all their former sexual partners and keep a check on their whereabouts, but to brief their children fully. In a sense, such a brief was like a map on which the parents had plotted all the oases they had found where the water was sweet in an otherwise hostile desert—a map without which a boy might get lost or even worse, on arriving at some distant village be regarded as a stranger and brutally molested.

Partners and pals

The trading partnership, however, as its name implies, had its commercial side, even though its ultimate function, like all other affiliations outside of the kinship group, was aimed primarily at bringing social stability to the society as a whole. As for the nature of the partnership, this depended to a great extent on the ecology of the region—on what the community lacked or had in plenty. In Alaska, for example, the nomadic tribes of the interior needed whale oil, ivory, sealskins and the like; the coastal tribes needed caribou and wolf skins from which to make certain items of clothing, and it made more sense to leave the procurement of these things to the specialist. So once a year at the great trading festival, the hunters would meet up with their trading partners to exchange goods of all kinds including their wives, and place orders for the following year. In this way the ecological boundaries were crossed and men from different tribes whose lives and livelihoods had nothing in common and who were perhaps even a little afraid and in awe of each other, developed a formal relationship which over the years would grow into a deep and lasting bond.

As with the trading partnerships between the nomadic and coastal Eskimos, so too with those that developed between hunters within their own ecological setting, a man would do his utmost to meet his partner's every request, even if in order to do so he had to deprive his own family. It was a matter of pride and, to some extent, of honour. The relationships in the case of the latter, however, were less formal partly because they met more often, but mainly, I suspect, because they had more in common.

Many Eskimo tribes had also a rather special relationship which fell somewhere between the ritualistic blood-brotherhood concept and that of the bosom pal. It was a relationship which grew out of their natural inclination to make fun, and usually developed among men who as boys had hunted together. With each other they could joke and play the fool without fear of causing offence for each regarded the other as his equal, and the mild insults and pranks with which they tormented each other were regarded by society

Physical beauty counted for little for it served no practical purpose, but this in no way distressed the girl that was prettier than the rest for although not vain she was well aware that beauty was a bonus to whatever other talents and virtues she possessed.

as an indication of the mutual esteem and "special" friendship which existed between them.

In Alaska there was a more formalized version of this relationship—a sort of older man's version where the two, if they lived a long way apart, would send each other songs which were intended, through their play on words and their unflattering remarks, to amuse, but at the same time to taunt their partner. The one who carried the song from one pal to the other would, of course, be coached by the composer until he was word perfect, and would be received at the village where he was to deliver the song with great excitement, for such songs were always the source of interest and entertainment to everyone in the community. With the song would always be sent a gift and the more insulting the verse the more worthwhile the gift had to be. Nevertheless, such song contests could get out of hand and so deeply offend one of the partners that the relationship would come to an end. This, however, rarely happened for the whole point of this relationship, as with all the others that the Eskimo took pains to develop, was to increase his circle of friends as far beyond the boundary of his kinship group as he was ever likely to travel.

The trading festival was a way in which the inland and the seacoast Eskimos in Alaska could exchange all kinds of goods and place orders for the following year. But commercial though these festivals were, they served also to strengthen the ties between individual trading partners and through the annual exchange of wives "unite" their children in a half-brother relationship which further increased the stability of the general social structure.

Another annual social occasion in Alaska was the celebration which marked the end of the whaling season. The culmination of this was the game of "sky tossing" in which everyone took part.

Crime and punishment

The verses delivered by the singing messenger from one song partner to another, although at times insulting, were essentially a form of good-humoured competition between the two composers and their object was mainly to amuse. This was not so between men from the same community who bore a grudge against each other, or where there was some more serious dispute to be settled between the two. In this case the whole community would assemble to hear the protagonists fight their duel, and the object here was to ridicule the opponent in order to tilt the balance of public opinion against him.

The judicial settlement by song was at its most effective in Greenland. It was used to a lesser extent in Alaska and not at all in the central region where disputes generally were settled with a bout of punching—each man taking it in turns to thump his opponent on the temples until one of them gave in or was knocked senseless by the blows. Justice was not served by these fights, but then, neither was there any justice in the settlement by songs. The two men, facing each other in the middle of a circle formed by the onlooking crowd, would take turns in making up

some slanderous and abusive lampoon about his opponent, which each in turn would chant and wail to the accompaniment of a drum. The listener was required to stand motionless and his face betray no hint of embarrassment or anger at the venomous remarks that were being made about him. Nor was he supposed to retaliate when his opponent during the singing of the song repeatedly smashed his skull into his face. But what counted for more than all the insults hurled by the singer at his silent victim was the cut and thrust of satire and the adroitness of the two men in countering the insults with some really filthy words and a sparkling display of wit—and the winner, of course, was the cleverer of the two, providing the constant clashing of heads had not crushed the sharper man's faculty for brilliant repartee.

What happened to the loser would depend to some extent on the individual and how much humiliation he had suffered in the contest. In some cases the teasing and baiting of the loser would be so merciless that he would have no alternative but to leave the district never to return, for with public opinion against him, he could no longer share in the life of the community. This was the law of the pack—a law not based on justice, but on the need for harmony. In a dispute between two men, one must lose before peace is restored and it did not seem to matter to the Eskimos whether the one that won was right or wrong as long as he lived in harmony with his fellows from that day on. If on the other hand the one who won was irascible and thoroughly anti-social, the long-suffering community would tolerate him for a while in the forlorn hope that he might improve then, one by one each family would leave the village, being careful to find some good excuse so as not to hurt the feelings of the one from whom they were fleeing.

Rarely did they plot collectively to rid themselves of some individual who was a menace to their community; but occasionally it was necessary as a last resort—say in the case of a maniac who had murdered several people, or someone who was known to be using witchcraft against them. Even then, it was not by way of punishment for these anti-social acts that they would ambush and kill their victim, but simply to restore some semblance of order to the community, for where there was fear or a breakdown of cooperation between the hunters or their women, their very existence was put in jeopardy.

First then among the unwritten laws of the Eskimo society was this: every man, woman and child had to contribute as fully as they were able to the never-ending struggle for survival. The good hunters were admired, the poor hunters pitied, and the thieving parasites despised; while among the women, the industrious were kept and the lazy thrown out to die or mend their ways. The old and weak were duty bound to release their frail hold on life when they could no longer feed

Although (within the kinship group) the Eskimo had built himself a wall—a fortress of extended kin behind which he could shelter from the hostile outside world—those who offered him protection in turn expected protection from him. So by taking three wives instead of one, as the East Greenland hunter in this picture had done, he on the one hand increased by two family groups those who would protect him; ironically by doing so he had become more vulnerable.

themselves, and infanticide was the accepted way in the more impoverished communities of keeping their numbers in check.

Somewhat surprisingly, there were no territorial claims: the hunting grounds were regarded as the property of everyone; but the food and skins brought in were shared according to a set of rules which varied from place to place. Nowhere in the Arctic, however, would a hunter amass more food than he could eat while others in the community had none. And in some respects, the same rules applied also to a man's personal possessions. A man, for example, could not inherit a skin boat if he already had one—he could, of course, keep the better of the two, but he was obliged to give away the one he could not use, just as he would naturally keep the best cuts of meat for his own family and friends, and give the offal to his dogs or to those in his community

Above and right: the hunter is making the delicacy kiviak, *by stuffing about 800 little auks into a sealskin sack and burying it under rocks. Dug out in winter, the blubber lining of the sack and the birds have combined to make the* kiviak, *which is eaten raw.*

who never hunted for themselves.

Seldom was there any serious friction between men over food or personal property, for a man as a rule would not debase himself by bawling out a thief—he would rather leave that to his wife who, in any case, had the sharper tongue. Even where the "property" stolen was the woman herself and a husband's honour was at stake, the Eskimo philosophy provided its own neat solution to a potentially dangerous situation by absolving the abductor of all blame, and heaping abuse on the unfortunate woman who had been the "cause" of her husband's shame. In this way, without further embarrassment, the husband could enter the house of the abductor and with the utmost civility retrieve his wife as he would a stray dog and vent his anger on a creature weaker than himself to his own enormous satisfaction and also, strangely enough,

to the deep-seated pride of his screaming wife, for had he not wanted her he could just as easily have saved face with his community by publicly announcing that the abductor, though a fool, had saved him the trouble of kicking her out.

So harmony once again is restored, but at the expense, it would seem, of justice, and everyone in the community is happy including the woman who had first been abused, then soundly thrashed, and now lay whining like a dog in the corner of her den. But unfair though it may seem to us, it was a social formula that worked. It was a behaviour pattern which had its roots in the most primitive of all human traits: man's natural and unquestioning submission to the authority of the pack, and that most basic of all survival instincts which warns that the only way to avoid trouble is to stay out of its way.

A man enjoyed prestige if he owned a boat, but was ridiculed if he owned two. The same applied to food where a hunter's prestige was not a measure of his skill but a measure of the amount of meat he gave away to those who were in need.

Opposite, below: one example of the abandonment of old ways in favour of those of the white man is that only at the summer camps will one still find people sharing.

43

CHAPTER FOUR

THE CYCLE OF LIFE

We have seen how the Eskimo society responded to the external stresses put upon it by the environment and by the odd discordant element which threatened to destroy it. We have seen too how the individual made use of his family, friends and trading partners, and how in turn he was used by them. But we need to see that society from within if we are fully to understand the man, for it was not his skill, his spirit or even his blood that made him Eskimo—it was that process which the anthropologist calls socialization; the process by which a society moulds the personality of each individual into a shape it is prepared to accept.

The methods and pressures, of course, vary greatly from one society to the next, for each has its own way of life and its own distinctive character. Even in a relationship as fundamental as that which exists between man and nature, you will find some societies that are conditioned from childhood to believe that everything which is part of the natural world can be controlled by man, and at the other extreme, societies such as the Eskimos who lived in constant fear of offending the *inue* or spirits of all the creatures, objects and phenomena with which they coexisted. But it would be a mistake to rate one society superior to another for there is simply no accepted standard by which they can be judged. How are we to say, for instance, which was the greater achievement: the mastery of the polar environment by the billion-dollar investment of modern man in equipment and supply lines, or the survival of the Eskimo in that same environment with nothing more than the meat, skin, bones and blubber of the animals he killed?

This much, however, is certain—by comparison with our own complex socialization, the Eskimo process of learning was simple, for all that was required of him in life was to provide. His course ran in a rut worn by the guiding ethics of his race—a course in which each twist and turn was a crisis in life that had been met at the same point in the cycle by countless generations of men who had passed that way before him. He was not required to compete with his fellow men in order to survive, for his was a social system in which "equality" was the basic principle of life—a system which tended to stifle originality and snuff out all but the brightest sparks of initiative; a system in which most people were so afraid of self-assertion that the only voice of authority outside the collective voice of public opinion was that of the *angákoq* or magician, and even his voice carried no weight unless,

Life according to the Eskimo was a recurring cycle in which death was merely nature's way of discarding a body that had grown old, for through its name the soul lived on.

The name that was given to the child was the soul of its previous owner. But the child also had a soul of its own and it was, the Eskimos believed, the union of these souls within the body of the child that gave the child its character.

believed, were made up of three elements: a body, a soul, and a name that was also a soul of sorts. The distinction between these two souls when the body was alive was so subtle that no Eskimo ever succeeded in explaining it to his own children let alone to the white man; but presumably they were united, for according to the Eskimos, when the soul was released from the body by death, it split into two separate entities—one soul going *down* to the Eskimo "Heaven" where it was warm and there was an abundance of game; the other remaining in torment here on Earth where it was inclined to intrude in the affairs of the living until it was called upon by name to enter the body of a new-born child.

Even in the European societies where the name is nothing more than a sound label which is stuck on the child for convenience, it is important that the name should be considered "acceptable" by the class of society into which the child is born. So you can imagine how much more serious the problem of choosing a name was for the Eskimos where each name was a soul that not only would influence the character of the child but indirectly would

in a state of trance, it was being used to relay a message directly from the "gods".

The taboos were something else—the "words" of authority if you like—and these could be passed on by anyone. But to see how they, the *angákoqs* and the power of public opinion affected and greatly complicated the lives of the Eskimos, let us follow the individual through the various stages of his life and observe his reactions to that process by which his society subtly shaped or forced him to conform.

The incomplete child

Unlike the young of all other animals, human babies, the Eskimos

affect the community as a whole. In fact, it was so important to the community that the choice was right, that pressure was often put on the parents to call in an *angákoq*, for even where some sign had been given to the parents through their dreams or through some manifestation of the dead in the behaviour of their infant and the *angákoq* was not needed to actually conjure its names, his magic powers still came in useful in keeping at bay the many undesirable souls that were "hanging around", each hoping to slip uninvited into the body of the baby through its anus and so set in motion the cycle of another life.

Here then, in the link between the living and the dead, is that sense of continuation on which the Eskimo based his peace of mind. Here too was his guarantee that the evil in man would not be perpetuated, for in his concept of reincarnation, only those among the dead who were remembered for their good qualities would be adopted for another term within another body.

I call this concept "reincarnation" merely for want of a better word for as I have already said, the soul of an Eskimo was not simply the soul inherent in his name. The body also had some kind of spirit of its own— one that must to some extent have been influenced by heredity—and it was the *union* of these two souls that gave the body life. Moreover, the concept drifts even further from the accepted idea of reincarnation with each additional name, and since a child was rarely given less than three, the mixture of qualities it absorbed was often so confusing that it was practically impossible to identify any of the original donors in the host personality.

Even so, the presence of those other souls within him still commanded respect for themselves. The tiny baby, for instance, who had been given the name of his deceased grandfather would immediately become the "father" of his own mother, and for this reason if for no other it was unthinkable that the child should ever be punished. As soon as the child was capable of reasoning it was necessary, therefore, to introduce him in the simplest terms to all those "within" and around him and to the relationships between them in order that he might not be confused when on occasions he was referred to as "grandfather" by his brothers, or

Sometimes several names would be given a child in order to combine the qualities of its many donors. For an old woman it was only natural that she should "see" in each gesture and expression of the children around her all the proof she needed that her belief was true.

as "husband" by the old woman who was his namesake's widow.

Similarly the child was introduced to the contents of the small skin sack which hung from a string around its neck: a raven's bill, an owl's claw, a tooth, a talon, a dried-out piece of umbilical cord, a feather or a tuft of hair—soot from a lamp or a caribou's ear—all chosen with great care because each item for the Eskimo was a "living" thing and possessed certain magic powers. These were his amulets or charms; but like his names, they had not been of his own choosing— they had been strung around his neck by the *angákoq* when the child was only a few days old, and it was important that he should now under-

With their friends, as with the puppies that share the playground of their world, children are encouraged to be considerate and kind, and through their games prepare themselves for the trials that lie ahead.

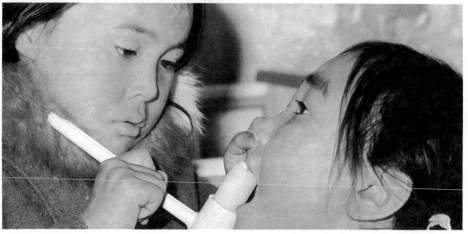

had to pay every time he made use of one of his protective powers. Not that this bothered the Eskimos much for they were as clever at creating antidotes as their forefathers had been at creating taboos, and they had any number of ways of building up their immunity to a particularly onerous rule.

Spells and magic songs they also regarded as "property" which could be bought, bartered or bestowed, but which if stolen would back-fire on the thief. And in some cases where a song and an amulet went stand that it was not so much the "things" themselves that would protect him, but the *inua* or spirit which each possessed.

There was, however, a limit to how many amulets a child might be given. There had to be, for almost anything could be used no matter how grotesque providing it symbolized some attribute which was considered essential to a man or useful to a woman, so they ruled that no two people wearing the same amulet could marry and this effectively restricted each person to two or three amulets at the most.

Then there were also the food taboos to be considered when making a choice of charms, for each amulet carried with it a restriction— a sort of penalty which the wearer together, the power was really potent for these songs were not hymns or a cry for help addressed to some benevolent God, but an attempt by man to control or divert the malevolent powers which threatened their existence. Each was a secret formula that worked only for its owner and the power of each song was specific. A hunter's insurance was therefore as big as his repertoire of magic, for without his spells and magic songs, his amulets and charms, and his carefully conjured set of names and their consortium of souls he was simply too vulnerable to go out into the world.

The growing game

Of course, if we could believe that

For the Eskimo boy there is no clear-cut dividing line between play and preparation for manhood, for every game or piece of gear which he might find around the house or down at the water's edge is something he must learn to handle if he is to become a hunter.

the soul of every Eskimo child was a composite of several "adults" this would explain a great deal: their patience for instance; their capacity to endure physical pain, and that extraordinary quality of mutual respect which existed between the parent and child. To the Western way of thinking, however, this soul-adopting concept is wholly unacceptable. So how then are we to account for the fact that Eskimo children, in spite of being indulged in almost every wish and never punished, were more respectful and obedient, more tolerant and better natured than the European child?

Among the Eskimos a new-born child was the centre of a circle made up by doting kin. The world revolved around him and the outstretched arms and cooing sounds and the mural of adoring smiles were accepted by him with the almost uncanny composure of one who "had been through it all before". It was scooped up every time it cried and pressed against a giant breast to suck and grow into a child, and the bursting of each bubble of wind set off a peal of laughter that would ring around the warm stone den like the echo of the laughing souls which were having a ball inside him. Every

twitch of its arms or sound it made was seen as a sign from those within, and every facial contortion recognized as the toothless grimace of one of its namesakes and further proof to the onlooking crowd that the best of the dead returned to Earth to show man the way to "Heaven".

Even when the infant grew tired and its souls all fell asleep, on the far side of the fleshy curtain it had drawn across its eyes the adulation of family and friends would rumble noisily on, for among the Eskimos there were no set hours for the expression of maternal love and no formal functions to attend at which the children played no part. Here the young were the privileged ones and the grown-ups merely the protectors, providers and teachers of a new generation of men. Here they could move from den to den and share freely in the food and warmth of any brood they chose without fear of being shown less affection in a neighbouring *igdlo* than in the one from which they had come. Their home was their village; their bed the nearest skin-covered platform on which they could find a space to lie down, and their solace when they were hurt or distressed, the comforting strength and sympathy of whichever adult picked them up and wiped away their tears.

But safe though they were within the crèche, this was no infant's paradise, for beyond the bleached bones and piles of blubber that marked the boundary of their world prowled all the fearsome animals they would one day have to hunt. They learned about them through their songs and through the fables they were told by the old folk of the village who were now too frail to travel far, and as they learned about the world and all the powers for

tribes to sit boy babies outside the *igdlo* naked when the north wind blew to be killed or toughened by the cold, and this was only the first test of many that a boy would have to undergo before its parents were satisfied that he had won the right to live. Throughout childhood and right on through adolescence into the uncertain maturity of every young hunter, boys walked in the shadow of men who were obsessed with their physical prowess, and hard, perhaps even inhumane though it may seem to us, a child in whom some frailty was detected, or

The techniques of hunting and balancing a kayak are learned from a very early age.

good and evil that would influence their lives, there grew between the young and old a very special bond, for the old were wise, the old were kind, but above all, the old had time on their hands to feed the daydreams of the young and a lifetime's experience on which to draw when answering the questions of the children in their care.

Not that the old were the only ones to influence or leave their mark on the character of the child. It was the custom among some Eskimo

worse—some incurable physical flaw—was sometimes rejected by the society as any pack of wolves would rid itself of an animal that was deformed or seemed in any way inferior to the rest. By culling the weak and training the strong not only to endure but actually to thrive on suffering, the Eskimos survived.

An Eskimo boy was taught to tread lightly and not raise his voice for loud noises would frighten the animals away and attract the attention of evil spirits that were out prowling in search of men. He was trained to control his desire for food, and for days on end to abstain from eating in order to shrink the size of his stomach and prepare him for the privations which he might as a luckless predator some day have to suffer. He was encouraged to develop his stamina and strength and to excel in every test he was set, and yet remain modest and circumspect. It was a virtue, he was told, to be generous and kind. A virtue to be considerate and co-operative with kin. It was a virtue to be industrious; a self-sufficient man—a man of iron self-discipline yet gentle as a lamb, and a virtue to be as peaceful and long suffering as a saint and many, many more besides, too numerous to mention, for the accepted ideal was a social being with the grace and integrity of a God and the virility of a ram.

Girls, by comparison, had an easier time for they had less to learn and much less to experience than the boys on whose skill as hunters they would all one day depend. But although childhood for them was freer in the early years of growing up, they, like the boys, were never allowed to lose sight of their allotted role. Even in the growing game in which the young played adult roles strictly according to their own vague concept of the rules, they drifted instinctively along the way towards what the society, not they, decided they should be, for socialization Eskimo-style could be every bit as subtle as it could at times be hard. A child, for instance, would be warmly applauded only for those achievements associated with its sex and mildly reproached for any skills it developed which taboos would later forbid it to use. But these rebukes and warnings were always tempered with words of

encouragement, and it is perhaps for this reason more than any other that Eskimo children felt a sense of well-being in the company of adults. They were a part of the adult world— a respected and increasingly more useful part of the kinship group to which they belonged, and consequently, once past puberty, of the society as a whole.

Puberty and the practical man

There must be a reason why the Eskimos did not make much of a

ritual out of puberty, and the only guess I can offer that seems in keeping with their concept of what qualities went to make a man is that no ritual, however dramatic, would make a single bit of difference to a boy who had not yet proved himself equal to the role. Of course, a boy's voice did not break without attracting some attention—nor for that matter did a girl's change of shape or the blush that came rushing to her cheeks when the change was pointed out; but among most tribes

By the time a boy is about 7 years old his relationship with his father has changed. It is as though he has suddenly become aware that his father is a hunter, and from that moment on he is in awe of him.

a boy's passage through puberty was marked by nothing more than a serenade of female sniggers and the odd crude male remark about his "ripening" condition.

True, there was a change in the style of clothing and a boy was permitted more often to join the men out hunting, but he was still very much the apprentice and would remain so for many years, for in the eyes of the Eskimos a boy was no more a hunter as a result of his first kill than he was a man the morning after he had hit a lower note.

With a girl it was different. By definition she became a woman at her first menstruation and was eligible for marriage from that moment on. The puberty rites for girls, however, were not so much a celebration of this change of status as a protection against it, for the taboos and restrictions to which a girl was subjected at this time were all bound up with the belief common among so many primitive peoples that a menstruating woman attracted the attention of evil spirits not only to herself, but in the case

There is less to learn and much less experience for the girls than for the boys on whose skill as hunters they will one day perhaps depend.

These girls would not be encouraged to ask how the whales on the beach were killed. For even today there is a strict division of labour between the sexes and neither is allowed to lose sight of its allotted role in life.

of the first menstruation, to the community as a whole.

In Alaska, for instance, she was confined for five days to the *igdlo* or den and obliged to wear a special hood of caribou skin which covered her eyes. She was not permitted to lift this hood and should she wish to urinate she had to be guided by another woman to a place well clear of the *igdlo* where the snow was pristine white and no animal, bird, or human being had left the faintest track or stain. She could not eat or touch raw meat, nor could she scrape or sew a skin without offending the *inue* of the animal concerned. She could not even look at a hunting weapon without rendering it useless from that moment on, and could drain the power out of any *angákoq* who came within a mile. In short, she was such a liability to everyone around her that it was as much a relief to the community at large as it was to the girl in question when finally her confinement came to an end and she sallied forth as a woman.

Needless to say, the puberty rites were much more rigorous

For the boy there is no initiation into manhood. He is introduced to the techniques of hunting first through stories, then through play and eventually by accompanying his father or an uncle on the shorter hunting trips.

among those tribes that were influenced by Indians: on the Aleutian Islands, for example, the period of seclusion was forty days during which time the girl could not even scratch her head without breaking a taboo. Nor was it merely by chance that the Eskimos clear of these influences settled for a simpler set of rules. As far as they were concerned, the demands of life were severe enough without the added complication of taboos that were impractical, and they applied this same principle to every step

There was for the Eskimos no "mystery" in sex, and therefore no virtue whatsoever in a girl remaining chaste. Nor were there any moral codes to disturb the conscience of the young who wished to play the field before choosing a mate for their first attempt at marriage. But as I have said earlier, we must be wary of this word "marriage" for among the Eskimos it was a purely practical relationship in which two people of the opposite sex joined forces in order to become a more effective unit in the struggle for

they took from the cradle to the grave. Indeed, so intensely practical were these people, their culture was almost totally lacking in that irrational element which we in the West call "romance".

Everything was reduced to its simplest terms. There was, for instance, no courtship ritual, little or no coquettishness, and in line with their philosophy that nothing had any value unless it was perfectly functional, they designed their clothing with the sole object in mind of keeping themselves warm.

survival. The relationship was not idealized and certainly not regarded as binding—in fact, it was considered most unusual for a couple to settle down to a lasting partnership before both parties had suffered the misery of at least two attempts at marriage that had ended in divorce. Consequently there was no stigma attached to the divorcee or to any children born of that union, or for that matter, to any offspring providing it was healthy.

There is, of course, nothing unusual in this, for there are parallels to be found for everything I have said in our own permissive society; but dig a little deeper and you will suddenly come across a totally alien culture—a male-dominated social structure in which the woman, although essential from an economic point of view, was forced to play the passive role as the property of man. True, in matters which affected her alone she made her own decisions and often without the slightest regard for what anyone else might think. She was free, for instance, to choose for herself whether or not to accompany her man should he decide to go on a long hunting trip or to move camp to another location, and even though her decision in this case directly affected not only her husband but the whole family group who were dependent on him for food, he would bring no pressure to bear on his wife or make any attempt to persuade her to go with him against her will. He would simply exchange her for the wife of a friend for the duration of the trip or for whatever length of time the two hunters felt the exchange was to their mutual satisfaction.

Whether the women were agreeable to the swap was never taken into account, for here it was a husband's right to dispose of his wife as he thought fit; he had after all been trained to provide and to make decisions that were in the best interests of the family as a whole. But it was still a piece of male chauvinism as far as the women were concerned, and as such provoked screams of derision, for even though they were well aware that the arrangement was a practical one, and an important one too as a social device for strengthening the bonds between the two families that were involved, it rankled that women were vulnerable to every

male whim and were regarded by society as subservient to men. So it was seldom the offending women would let the moment of exchange slip by without turning the whole village into a stage for a ranting drama that would echo up and down the coast for months or even years.

The fact is, the Eskimo loved a good story, and an opportunity to take the stage as its central figure was impossible for them to resist, especially when the theme of the story was as old as mankind itself.

The missionaries did not fully succeed in shattering the old folk's peace of mind, for the alternatives they offered to being reborn an Eskimo was a Heaven full of white men or a Hell which to the pagan could hardly have seemed much worse.

To have drawn attention to themselves purely to satisfy their own vanity would have exposed them to ridicule. But this was different. This was an ear-splitting ritual struggle against the men that were molesting them and clearly set on raping them, or even worse, ignoring them and they were expected to put on a good show with plenty of action and histrionics, for it was the details of the story that would give it the staying power to travel right along the coast: the characters and their choice of words; the blow-by-blow description of the way each woman was brutally dragged kicking and biting to the sledge, and how their outraged cries were still being heard long after the hunters and their seemingly reluctant cargos had disappeared from view. Indeed, so noisy and dramatic were these protests that the real abductions by comparison often looked like elopements. And this, come to think of it, was just as well, for when a man's honour was at stake it was safer for everyone around if he put the blame on his wife.

The system, of course, would never have worked had there been any strong emotional ties between a man and wife; but there was little fear of the system collapsing on account of this, for although there was often a deep bond of affection between the older married couples, there was no dialogue of shared ambition, no silent exchanges of the mind or intimacy of any sort between the younger ones except on a sexual level. The culture simply made no provision for the expression of a person's "feelings". Only with his

Romantic love was not and is still not extolled by the Eskimos and although it exists between some couples, more commonly the relationship between a man and his wife lacks those strong emotional ties that are formed between two people of compatible intellect. Among the old folk of course the bond is much deeper, but even they will rarely confess to each other their fears or their innermost thoughts.

Throughout childhood and right on through adolescence into the uncertain maturity of every young hunter, boys walked in the shadow of men who were obsessed with their physical prowess. They were encouraged to develop their stamina and strength, and to excel in every test they were set and yet to remain modest and circumspect.

closest friends could an Eskimo unwind, and even then he was not free to admit his fears or to confess to having heard the voice that murmured in his soul.

Intellectually he was thus made impotent by the very virtues he extolled, for although his conversation was always cheerful, his sense

of propriety dictated that it should be superficial, and any tensions that he as a hunter was unable to release by the act of killing or by tanning the hide of his wife, he was expected to repress. In fact, had it not been for the Eskimo's infectious and irreverent sense of humour and his passionate love of life, it seems unlikely that they, for all their skill and ingenuity, would have made the grade. But these two characteristics were the counterweights for the whole unstable system. They affected everything he did and his relationship with everything with which he coexisted: his love of life provided him with the incentive to survive, whilst his sense of humour served as a sort of panacea for all his ills and a tonic for his soul.

The parting of the souls

But this love of life, if it is to be properly understood, must be seen in the light of the Eskimo's vague but strangely beautiful beliefs about what happened to his soul at death— so too should the instinct which

Eskimo children, generally speaking, were little affected by divorce—for the scene as far as they were concerned was essentially the same. They were loved no less, nor were they in the social sense without a home and parentless for the pack, in spite of an occasional reshuffle, invariably remained intact.

impelled the old folk to commit suicide when they felt they were becoming a burden on their kin. It was also influenced by his "intimacy" with death, for not only did he face death almost every day of his life, but as a hunter he dispensed it.

He killed, of course, strictly according to the sanctions imposed upon him by the animals themselves, for it was his belief that by observing the rules and treating each carcass with the utmost respect, the animals he had killed would be reborn and would allow themselves to be killed again by him or by his sons. His own death too he believed would be a transition into something new— no better perhaps than his present existence, but certainly no worse. So although everywhere in the Eskimo area a profound fear seized the living in the presence of the dead, and there existed the most

Most of the larger settlements these days can provide accommodation for the old folk in a "home" where, with dignity and serenity, they can see out their twilight years.

exact rules as to how a dead person's kin were to conduct themselves when a member of the family had passed on; as far as the dying were concerned, the spectre of death offered them a release from their frail and futile hold on life and it was the custom of the Eskimos gladly to accept it—even to the extent of suicide.

In some tribes an old man would ask his eldest son or a well-loved daughter to assist him with his suicide, and it was rarely that an old man's request was refused even in matters as traumatic as this. These assisted suicides, however, would not be carried out until the conditions were right, and a suitable occasion might be at the height of a party when the whole family were gathered together and everyone was feeling replete and in a happy frame of mind. At such a moment the *angákoq* would get to his feet and purge the place of the evil spirits that had crowded in at the scent of death; then, with the ritual preparations completed, he would hand the executioner a special thong of skin which the chosen one would place around the neck of the old man. Sometimes it was quick; sometimes the whole thing was so distressing that the execution would have to be postponed for several hours or even days until in a state of emotional exhaustion the son would toss the trailing end of the sealskin thong over a beam, rub noses with the old man for one last time, then hoist him to his death. It was customary at this moment for everyone to come forward and lend the executioner a hand, or at least as a token of respect to sit on the free end of the rope at the other end of which hung a man and by this gesture share the responsibility for the old man's death equally among them.

Old women, it is said, usually preferred to die by the knife or to be abandoned when the family moved camp to another place, but of course many died peacefully by natural causes. Then there were murders, famines, diseases and witchcraft and any number of ways by which an Eskimo might lose his life while out travelling or hunting. But no matter what the cause or circumstance of a death, its effect on the family of the deceased was equally devastating.

In East Greenland, only the closest relatives were permitted to touch the dead, and immediately after the funeral they had to destroy all their clothing and replace it with new. Meanwhile, the man who had actually laid out the corpse and had been obliged to remain in its oppressive presence alone for three days would have to undergo a series of purifying rituals before he could hunt again. But these were nothing compared with the unbelievably severe restrictions imposed on a woman who might have been called upon to do the same job: for one whole year she remained "unclean" and was forbidden to look up, smile or speak above a whisper, or to mention the names of any animals of the hunt or to eat their meat.

The Eskimos seem to have been very much more practical when it came to disposing of the body. In the Canadian Arctic, for example, the dead were simply left out on the tundra some distance from the camp as food for the wolves. In some parts of Greenland they were left on the beach below the high-water mark to be carried away by the sea. Only on the Aleutian Islands and among the Pacific Eskimos of Alaska were the dead embalmed after a primitive fashion and "sat" in deep crevices in the rocks where it was less likely that they would be got at by the foxes and wolves.

In general then, although a death in the family interrupted the normal routine of life and stirred up a feeling of uneasiness amongst them, they did not over-indulge themselves in morbid speculation. They were more occupied with solving such problems that were to them of immediate and practical concern.

In the days before it was made law that all loose dogs would be destroyed, shallow graves were often desecrated by the dogs that roamed around in packs.

CHAPTER FIVE

THE RITUAL OF SURVIVAL

The Eskimo, as we have seen, was physically, socially and temperamentally geared to living in a harsh environment and a weakness in any one of these three would have tipped the balance against him. But there were two other elements in the culture which I believe were even more vital, for not only did they have a more direct bearing on his struggle for survival, but they were the very essence and purpose of the aboriginal hunter's existence.

These two elements—his technique of hunting and what is loosely called his religion—were in effect two sides of the same problem—namely, his relationship with the animals that were his source of food. Skill alone was not enough when it came to procuring game and neither was the most comprehensive repertoire of magic songs to a hunter who was lacking in expertise. Only by combining skill with ritual could he hope to be successful, for one of the basic concepts of his religion was that all animals were endowed with the ability to reason, talk, and react in much the same way as men. And not only did animals have a profound distaste for the fumbling incompetent, but they were not prepared even to favour the most assiduous of hunters except in response to cajolery, bribes and magic songs and a pattern of human behaviour which at times

was so obsequious that had the hunter had more self-respect, all his fawning would have made him sick.

The Eskimo's attitude towards religion, however, was more practical than philosophical, and so far as it related to the quest for food it had two well-defined objectives: to persuade the animal to come in the first place, and having come—to permit itself to be killed. Moreover, it would be reborn and would allow itself to be killed again only if its carcass had been treated by the hunter with respect and its severed head had been given a drink to quench its raging thirst. If, on the other hand, the hunter had been offensive or had failed in the smallest detail to observe the ritual sanctions, the animal would withdraw its favours and never appear again to that particular hunter, or worse, might even spread the word among all the others of its kind that this man and his kin, and perhaps the entire community from which this man had come, should be blacklisted by the species.

Much of what is generally termed the aboriginal religion thus lay in the attempts by man to please or appease the animals on whom his life depended, and to exert some measure of control over the supernatural world through ritual, magic and to lesser extent through com-

The Eskimo's struggle for survival was as much a religious preoccupation as it was a test of his skill and ingenuity.

munal religious rites. But from the very fact that the Eskimo needed some sort of religious concept to explain his fluctuating fortunes and the scarcity of game, it is clear that his power to affect control over the natural and supernatural world was strictly limited, and that as a predator he was more vulnerable in a spiritual sense than his prey.

Without the conviction that he could exert some measure of control over the supernatural world, the Eskimo would never have dared to venture out in the dead of winter. Had he not been able to do so he probably would not have survived.

If lucky, the hunter could in the autumn catch enough meat to last right through the long polar night. But these caches were often many miles from his village and could not be retrieved until the sea had frozen and he could fetch the meat by sledge.

Here then we have the rationale for the Eskimo's need for the shaman or *angákoq* as the Eastern tribes called the magician. He was the intermediary between man and the world of the spirits—a religious practitioner whose main function it was to determine who had violated a taboo, and through his helping spirits to restore some semblance of order and mutual trust between man and his sky full of gods.

Dwarfs, mermen and monsters

Until as recently as 160 years ago there were still a few isolated Eskimo tribes who believed they were the only human beings on Earth. In their search for food, however, they had never been alone; competing with them were supernatural beings that were both capricious and hostile, and best left strictly alone. Co-existing with them in the main was easier than it was with most of the true supernaturals, for men rarely came in contact with these strange beings.

Dwarfs were especially mischievous and even to this day are still seen in Alaska from time to time. They are described as being about one foot tall and look and dress like Eskimos. What's more they speak Eskimo fluently and sing very well and according to some reports, do a very good imitation of a howling wolf; but unlike human beings, they live in houses under the ground. How the Eskimos knew where they lived is a mystery, for according to the folklore and all recent reports, dwarfs vanish when they are chased or when a stone is hurled at them, and all tracks that have been followed have led eventually to the sea. On the whole though, they were fairly innocuous and so too, surprisingly enough, were the giants.

True, the further east one goes, the more aggressive these giants seem to have been and as I have said earlier, it was probably the people of the Dorset culture that were the *Tunit* of the legends. In Alaska, however, they were really rather timid and being of a somewhat reclusive nature they seldom bothered men. As for their height, you will find no figures in the folklore, and no monsters have recently been encountered, but is is generally agreed that they were "men" and that they grew in size the longer they were left alone.

Then there was a creature that had the body of a seal and the face and hair of a human being, and this had to be treated with the greatest respect by any hunter who discovered it entangled in his net. Very few in fact were actually seen for they were only found in the dead of winter. It was the custom for the cautious hunter to plunge his hand into the icy water to feel the face of the seal he had snared before hauling it on to the ice. If it had

The Eskimo had both a fear and a fascination of monsters. Even today the tupilak *carvings are a common subject among the Greenland artists.*

long hair and its face felt "human" the hunter would release the creature at once, for if he failed to do so he would surely die.

Strangely enough, the Eskimos gave it no name of its own—they simply called the creature *inuk*, a person, the same word they used to describe themselves, so clearly they classed it as something special. And special indeed it was, for although it never spoke to man, it could understand every word he said, and it was customary for the hunter when he had fully recovered from his shock to ask the creature to return as a seal, or the following spring as a walrus or a whale, and this it would do as a sign of its gratitude to the hunter who had released it. The creature was thus vindictive only if the rules were

broken, and since this was the basis of all relationships between man and the supernatural, virtually every act of the individual had some magical implication.

It is hardly surprising that Christianity was slow to catch on among the Eskimos, for it had first to destroy the aboriginal belief that the supernatural was natural. Even today in the Thule District of northwest Greenland where pastors have replaced the missionaries because they ran out of pagans, there are many Eskimos who still feel the power in nature which they have been taught does not exist.

The rule of land and sea

In the aboriginal Eskimo culture there came with the change of season a change too in the whole complex sphere of religious ritual. It shifted from that aimed at propitiating the mammals of the sea to that aimed at winning respect from the animals of the land, and the strictest of regulations kept the two apart.

In the western Arctic this concept was less pronounced than it was elsewhere. In Alaska, for instance, it was considered sufficiently respectful when eating land foods and seafoods at the same meal merely to wash the hands between courses; but among the central tribes, the most elaborate precautions had to be taken at the change of season to smoke all hunting weapons and clothing made of caribou over a fire of seaweed "to take away the smell of the land" before sealing or whale hunting could begin. Failure to take this precaution or to observe the many other taboos against mixing foods or activities inevitably brought revenge from one group or the other: either the game would stay away and the people would starve, or the community would be stricken with some dreadful sickness or hit by terrible storms. And it was at times such as these that the *angákoq* was essential to the community for it was only he, through his cultivated rapport with the spirit world, who was in a position to save them from total annihilation.

There were, of course, numerous other food taboos that were quite unrelated to this land and sea dichotomy. In fact, each animal had its own set and the more important the animal, the more elaborate were the restrictions the hunter had to remember. The proper treatment of animals thus became a fearful obsession every bit as hazardous as tiptoeing through a minefield, for although all hunters as children had been taught the rules of the game,

in the excitement of the hunt and the elation of success they were easy to forget. Now, as I have said earlier, all animals could speak Eskimo when they felt inclined, and much misery might have been averted had they been inclined to do so more often. But so seldom did they warn a man that he was heading straight into trouble that the shock of hearing the animal speak invariably caused him more consternation than the danger he had been warned to avoid.

In Alaska this was especially so, for there, when an animal was about to speak, the skin of its

muzzle rolled back to reveal a grotesque human face. Even dogs— the only animals that had no souls— were capable of doing this, and an example comes to mind of a man from Barrow, who not very long ago was driving his dogs so hard and beating them so mercilessly that the lead dog rolled the skin back off its face and asked the man why he was being so cruel—at which the man is alleged to have fainted and fallen off his sledge.

Blessed are the meek

Supreme though he was among predators, the Eskimo was by far the most vulnerable, and had he not seen the sense in this paradox he simply would not have survived. Even the most skilful and ingenious

The taboo is now a thing of the past, but even today the Eskimo is wary lest he should offend the inue of the animals he hunts.

among them were obliged to defer to every animal they killed and were in constant fear of violating some primeval law of nature. But he was not too proud to be prudent and in relation to animals this was his saving grace.

When a hunter, for instance, went out to his fox traps, he would always take with him those objects which he knew would appease the spirit of any animal he had caught—a needle and an ivory thimble for the female; a hunting knife for the male. These he would tie to the carcass of the animal before he took it home, and they would be removed after the head had been cut off and the carcass of the fox had thawed sufficiently for the woman of the house to skin it. It was also the custom when the head was cut off to ask the spirit of the fox to return, and this it would do if the hunter had treated it well. If on the other hand the hunter had been careless or disrespectful, the fox's spirit would hang around the house and cause all manner of misfortunes.

Wolves required the same sort of offerings and were treated in much the same way; but besides the more commonly used traps, the Eskimos devised an ingenious method by which a fifteen-centimetre, (six-inch) length of whalebone, sharpened at both ends, was bent and frozen into a lump of suet. When the wolf took the bait, the suet would thaw inside its stomach and release the sprung bone which would kill it. Magic songs were sometimes sung over such traps at the time they were set, and since the wolf was spiritually more dangerous than the fox there were certain food taboos that had to be observed after one had been killed. There were taboo restrictions too on taking more than five wolves at any one time, and this applied to all the smaller animals that were valuable for their pelts. No taboos, however, limited the number of caribou that might be taken at the seasonal hunt, and this is just as well for the caribou were a vital source of food not only to the inland tribes, but also to the Eskimos who lived at the coast.

This is not to say the Eskimos

The traditional game of spearing-the-peg, like so many of the games once played by the Eskimos, was designed to sharpen the skill and reflexes of the hunter and his sons. The object of this particular game was to pierce with a lance a tiny hole in an ivory toggle suspended between the floor and the ceiling by a tightened length of thong.

On thin sea ice and many miles from land a hunter throws out a line and manak —*a pear-shaped ball of wood in which some hooks have been set. Thrown beyond the seal he has shot, the hunter can haul in his line, hook the seal and pull it in to the edge of the ice.*

were given a free hand in the case of the caribou—on the contrary, there were many quite elaborate taboos associated with this animal. Mostly, though, they were related to how the carcass should be treated and, surprisingly enough, to the behaviour of children. Throughout the entire period that the hunters were away—a period in some cases of several weeks—the children were forbidden to walk on bare ground or to speak above a whisper; but had to remain in the *igdlo* or den where caribou skins had been laid on the floor as a carpet to deaden the sound. Tiresome for the children though this must have been, it was a discipline which clearly served them in good stead as hunters later on in life when patience and stealth were the prerequisites of every successful hunt.

Of course, the attributes required of a good hunter were many and varied. Some he acquired as a result of disciplines such as the rule of silence mentioned above, or the one referred to earlier by which he was trained to control his desire for food by shrinking the size of his stomach. Others, like the basic skills of hunting, required not only years of practice but a considerable measure of talent; and there were yet others that no amount of training could polish, for they were facets of his personality that would throughout his life flash brilliantly or remain forever dull—and one of these was courage.

The brown bear respected nothing else. According to the Eskimos he was the most intelligent of animals and endowed with tremendous power. No magic was a match for his spiritual strength and more than anything else he resented being killed by a man who was lacking in courage. Needless to say he was seldom offended, for only a man

with courage would take on a brown bear single-handed and fight him with a knife, and such was the respect of the bear for a man who was brave or rash enough to fight him that if the man was badly mauled but had succeeded in killing the bear, he had one certain cure for his wounds—he would wrap himself in the skin of the bear and very soon would recover. But no man ever boasted about killing a brown bear, and no man even mentioned the bear by name without risking his revenge. The taboos associated with his killing had to be carefully observed if those who in any way had been involved were to come away unscathed.

The polar bear, according to the Alaskan Eskimos, was weaker than the brown bear, but this "weakness" was conceptual—the brown bear's power could be transferred to humans, especially shamans, whereas the power of the polar bear could not. It was a match, nevertheless, for the bravest hunter and the skin of the polar bear is used even to this day by the Polar Eskimos of northwest Greenland. But spiritually powerful though it was, aside from cutting off its head to release its spirit and giving the animal fresh water to drink, there were no special rituals, no gifts or even requests made of the great white bear among the Alaskan Eskimos. One can only suppose this is because as a source of food it played a less significant role in the life of these tribes than the seals, walrus and whales on whom they seem to have devoted a good deal more ritual attention.

This was not the case in other parts of the Arctic. Among the Polar Eskimos the bear's head was placed on a window-sill facing towards the centre of the room and decorated with a harpoon line and a few pieces of blubber, meat and skin of a seal which, it was believed, would please the dead bear's soul. The Netsilik Eskimos did this too, but in addition brought the whole to the culture than the practice of giving the carcass a drink.

It was customary in Alaska, for instance, for the wife of the hunter to offer a cup of fresh, cold water

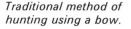

Traditional method of hunting using a bow.

Above right: the Polar Eskimo needs the bear not only for its skin, but as a challenge through which to reaffirm his courage and his skill. The same can be said of the walrus and, to a lesser extent, the narwhal. But only with the solitary wandering bear does the Eskimo sense an affinity.

hide into the *igdlo* and suspended it from a beam fur side out, filling the "sack" with various parts of its own insides such as its bladder, spleen and genitals as well as various other "gifts".

More widespread in the Eskimo area was the practice of throwing some part of the marine animal back into the sea—in some cases as an offering to the soul of the dead animal; in others in the belief that the part returned to its natural element would be reborn. With the first seal a boy killed, it was necessary to collect together all the bones and return them to the sea at the exact spot where the seal had been killed. The seal's soul would be well pleased by this gesture and favour the boy by returning to be killed by him time and time again. Similarly, in some parts of the Arctic the skull of the first polar bear a hunter had killed would be lowered into the sea. But no ritual was more common

to every seal her husband brought home. Here a special bowl made of wood or pottery was used for this purpose; elsewhere in the Arctic, however, the hunters or their wives were less particular about what sort of receptacle was used so long as the dead animal got its drink. Sometimes it was sufficient simply to soak a lump of snow in water and place it in the animal's mouth; but whatever form this ritual took, the custom of giving the animal a drink was considered an essential duty if good relations were to be maintained with the creatures of the sea.

Most Eskimo tribes also observed special taboos regarding the work done by women when marine animals were brought home in order not to offend Sedna, the old woman of the sea—the same woman who in Greenland is called *Arnaquagssâq*, for it was she who sent the marine animals out to be caught by men.

The taboos varied according to the type of mammal and the particular tribe concerned: small seals as a rule simply required that the woman did no work until the seal had been flensed; but with the larger animals, such as the bearded seal, walrus, narwhal and white whale, the restrictions on work might last for several days.

The larger whales, however, such as the bowhead or Greenland whale and the various types of fin whale (many of which exceeded eighteen metres [sixty feet] in length), provided such a bountiful supply of meat, bone and oil that the rituals and ceremonial surrounding them became so magnified and elaborate and so communal in concept that a whole cult built up around them. But complex though these rituals were—and far too involved to be included here—in the final analysis, the same general attitudes applied to the whale as they did to all other animals that were a part of the Eskimo's life: namely, that the whale allowed itself to be taken providing all pre-conditions and ritual sanctions had been respected, and every detail of equipment, item of apparel, chant, charm and sentiment of the hunters and their wives combined to please the whale and appease its soul in death.

Without exception, then, all the ritual and ceremonial behaviour of the Eskimo, in so far as it related to the animal world, was aimed at ensuring a steady flow of food, fuel and materials to support his life and the lives of his dependents. Since in the main it was the responsibility of each individual to maintain his good relationship with the animals he hunted and, as far as he was able, with the powers that controlled them, his struggle for survival was as much a religious preoccupation as it was a test of his skill and ingenuity.

As a challenge, the larger whales were of course in a class apart. Even hauling the carcass ashore was a relatively easy task by comparison with the hunt itself.

CHAPTER SIX

THE ART OF
KEEPING WARM

Underlying every Eskimo act was a rhythm of which his intellect was totally unaware, for the driving force of this vital rhythm was the cosmic force of repetition—the ordered cycle of his existence as a minute and yet very sensitive part of the complex of planets and the sun that we call the solar system.

But this sensitivity of the Eskimo was not some rare quality peculiar to him, nor was it limited only to the higher forms of life. The fact is, *every* living organism which depends for its survival on its ability to "sense" the time of day and the season of the year, has its own cyclical rhythms which are programmed to synchronize with others of its species and those seasonal shifts of light and heat that are natural to its environment. In species that migrate over enormous distances, these rhythms of course are more complex than in those that remain throughout the year a short distance from the place where they were born. And these rhythms, once established, take a very long time to adjust themselves to a different set of conditions.

Even man, who in the last two million years of his evolution has wandered all over the face of the Earth, is still essentially a simple semi-tropical creature conditioned by his internal rhythms to sleeping by night and working by day. He is thrown out of phase if he is transported too quickly east or west. His internal rhythms are even more confused if he is flown to the polar regions where the sun never sets in summer and where in winter it is dark in the higher latitudes for as much as five months of the year.

Now give man the choice of daylight or darkness, and invariably he will take the sun. Give him the choice of being hot or cold and he will move towards that source of energy that will sustain his life, for this is man's instinctive response to his internal rhythms and no intellectual argument will make much impression upon them. The Eskimo, however, was different, for on finding that the only solution to surviving in the frozen north was to regard the dark period as his dominant season and the sea with its treacherous skin of ice as his "natural" element, he not only managed to adapt to this harsh setting, but in the process produced the most distinctive and brilliant hunting culture that the world has ever known.

In a word

Of the techniques and equipment that he used I have time only to mention a few, and the subject even thus reduced is still at first glance confusing for there were among

In a cold environment clothing is more important than fire and no less important than food.

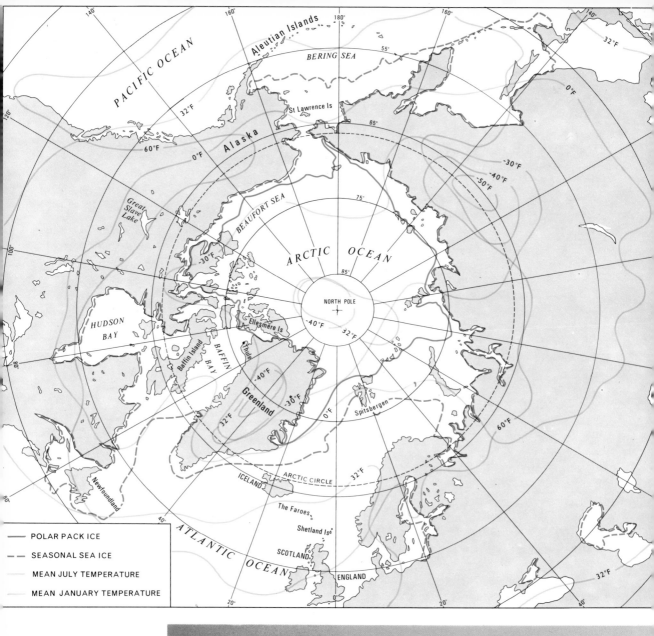

PACIFIC OCEAN

Aleutian Islands

BERING SEA

St Lawrence Is

Alaska

Great Slave Lake

BEAUFORT SEA

ARCTIC OCEAN

NORTH POLE

HUDSON BAY

Baffin Island

BAFFIN BAY

Ellesmere Is

Thule

Greenland

Spitsbergen

Newfoundland

ICELAND

ARCTIC CIRCLE

The Faroes

Shetland Is

SCOTLAND

ATLANTIC OCEAN

ENGLAND

60°F

32°F

0°F

-30°F

-40°F

-50°F

-30°F

-40°F

-30°F

0°F

32°F

60°F

32°F

40°

20°

—— POLAR PACK ICE

– – – SEASONAL SEA ICE

——— MEAN JULY TEMPERATURE

——— MEAN JANUARY TEMPERATURE

these arctic nomads as many variations on the cultural theme as there were camps of extended kin.

From east to west they ranged across at least 10,000 kilometres (6,000 miles) of what to the European eye would have seemed like total desolation, and from the shores of the polar sea in some places less than 800 kilometres (500 miles) from the North Pole, to "tribal" hunting grounds so far south that they stretched like fingers on the map deep into the Temperate Zones. And yet, with the exception of the Caribou tribe west of Hudson Bay and the inland tribes of Alaska who lived not only out of sight, but out of sympathy with the sea, the same *general* techniques of survival recurred throughout the whole vast territory. For although each group had its own mode of life and its own distinctive character, they all drew on the same mythology and the same fund of practical knowledge.

This would not have been the case had they been a settled people, but being a nomadic race, their techniques travelled with them until from the Bering Strait to the Greenland Sea there was a common method if not a common skill; a technique of survival that was known to every man—a sort of encyclopaedic knowledge from which a hunter might make use of only one small section in the course of his lifetime, but absorb it all he had to in order that this "heritage" could be handed on to his sons.

Small chance have we then of learning much about these techniques in a few hundred printed words! All we can do is to look for the key to their success, and this I believe you will find in a word that will never seem as apt again when applied to other men, for of all the talents the Eskimo possessed, none were more impressive than his INGENUITY.

Of course, it is a very human attribute—this ability to contrive, and one cannot fairly compare one culture with another without first taking into account the state of their technology and the materials they had to hand. By the same token, one should also avoid the temptation of labelling a people "primitive" merely because by some loose definition they were a Stone Age culture.

The Eskimo is a case in point. Try to find a place for him in the cultural evolution of mankind as a whole and one is bound to admit that (until quite recently) he had con-

The Eskimo was a traveller long before it occurred to him to domesticate the wolf-dog and hitch a few of them to his sledge. But the cultural effect of this discovery was the mastery of his environment.

tributed little or nothing to the intellectual or technical advancement of man since the discovery in the Middle East some 10,000 years ago of a bread wheat that could not propagate or yield without a little help. This is when civilization began. This is when man for the first time discovered that there was an alternative to the nomadic life, and one does not have to have read any history to know that he chose the alternative.

But the Eskimo never had this choice. He was totally remote from the progressive development of the rest of mankind. He lived at the very edge of the habitable world— a treeless, treacherous, frozen world in which the slightest change of climate could alter the whole balance of life. In order to survive he not only had to adapt to a climate and a latitude for which he was ill-equipped, but he had to make better use of his ingenuity than any other race. And so there evolved a "primitive" that was in a class apart, for without the knowledge, the materials, or the creative stimulus that comes from frequent contact with other cultural groups, the only outlet for his talents lay in refining every tool and technique that was a part of his heritage.

The second-hand skin

In most aboriginal cultures the equipment of survival was the wea-

The southern boundary of the Eskimo's territory was the northern limit of trees. But there was no obvious northern boundary for the Arctic Ocean, which covers over 12 million square kilometres (5 million square miles), is without a single feature that remains unchanged or in the same position from one day to the next.

How far the Eskimos ventured from the coast could depend on the state of the ice and the set of wind and current. But even the most experienced hunters were occasionally caught out and would, unless they had some way of converting a sledge into a boat, find the odds against getting back stacked heavily against them.

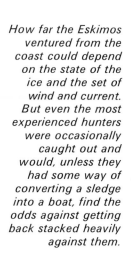

pon and the craft. Clothing played only a minor part if it played any part at all. But among the arctic peoples it was more important than fire and no less essential than food. For unlike all other forms of life that were obliged to stay strictly within the limits that nature had imposed, man in his wisdom had discovered that he could push back these boundaries and live anywhere on the face of the Earth providing that he could find enough food and could protect his body from the cold. And so he had dressed himself in second-hand skins, and after a little experimenting had settled for a style and a range of clothing best suited to the climate that he lived in.

It was, of course, by no stroke of luck that the Eskimo found himself with a choice of some of the warmest furs in the world, for every animal he skinned was perfectly protected against the cold. Arctic animals, however, are equipped each according to its size and the thickness of that layer of fat or blubber which they all carry beneath their skin, so the properties of the fur varies greatly from one animal to another.

The skin of the harp and ringed seals is strong and if properly treated is almost waterproof—an ideal material for covering *kayaks*; for making *kamiks*, the Eskimo's boots; his mitts, anoraks and many other things; but as clothing it is warm enough only for use in summer. Bear skin on the other hand, although not so tough, has a hard-wearing fur which is exceedingly warm and the Polar Eskimos even to this day still use this skin for making their trousers and winter *kamiks*. This skin, however, is too

The misery of the ice in thaw was the price the traveller had to pay for straying too far from home. By June the floes were flooded with water, and by the time it had drained away about the middle of July exposing beds of candle ice as sharp as forests of splintered glass, no Eskimo hunter in his right mind was still out on the ice.

Sea-ice travel was safest in the months of February and March, for shortly after the return of the sun the temperature was at its lowest and open leads and fractures in the ice would freeze over within a few hours.

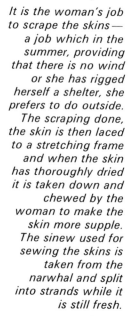

heavy for the parka, so this they made from fox, wolf or caribou skins and even here, where the Eskimo had three skins that were suitable, there were big differences between them: fox skin is supple, light, a delight to wear and very warm—but too fragile to wear on a long, hard journey; wolf skin is tougher and of the three is the best compromise between comfort and warmth; but if warmth is the only consideration and you don't mind the constant rain of hairs that fall into everything you eat and drink, then caribou is the answer.

The Eskimos have a saying that you are not a man until you have eaten your own weight in caribou hair, and that about sums it up, for by the time an Eskimo boy was eighteen he might just about qualify.

As for the reason why caribou hair sheds, this becomes obvious when you fish them out of your soup: every hair is hollow and in consequence breaks off easily—in fact it may even have been this cavity in the hair which gave the Eskimo his solution to the problem of keeping warm. To make up for his lack of blubber the Eskimo had to think of an alternative that was not only a poor conductor of heat but was also light in weight—and air, of course, was his answer.

He wore two layers of clothing, sometimes three, and each was so loosely fitting that there was room for the air that was warmed by his body to circulate freely inside the cocoon of fur that formed his outer layer. His innermost layer would be of bird skin, hare or eider duck, and the great advantage of all these skins over the garments he uses today was that his skins could "breathe". A man could be saturated with sweat but within a few minutes it would all have evaporated through his furs and condensed and frozen in the guard hairs of his outer parka. All he had to do then was beat out the frost with a stick.

The disadvantage with furs was the time put into making and repairing them. They had to be dried out

thoroughly at the end of each day and great care taken, especially with the more fragile skins, to stitch up the tiniest tear. *Kamiks* were perhaps the worst chore of all, for these were made up of an inner boot of dog skin and an outer boot of seal, caribou or bear—the two separated by an insole of dried grass underfoot and an air space around the calf. To keep the outer boot supple it had to be first thoroughly dried then worked hard over a blunt-edged blade at the end of a stout stick. It was to perform chores such as this and cook his food, rather than for her company, that the hunter preferred to take his wife with him whenever he went on a long hunting trip—or someone else's wife if his own was indisposed or in an uncooperative mood.

Some variety in style of clothing is only to be expected considering the vastness of the territory occupied by the Eskimo; but essentially all these styles were based on the same

Left: the dried sinew or ivaloo *can be softened by moistening it between the lips. It is far better than cotton or nylon thread for sewing skins as it does not "saw" the skin when the seams of the garments are worked.*

In style of clothing the Eskimos' gear varied greatly but the principle was always the same—to insulate themselves by using two or three layers of animal fur to trap two or three layers of air.

Among most tribes a man's status was a measure of his skill as a hunter and the strength of his kinship group. In the western Arctic, however, a man's

general principle of several loose-fitting layers with caribou as the main winter skin. The hooded parka in the Hudson Bay region reached almost to the knees and had slits up each side and a fringed hem; in the North-West Passage it looked like

a badly fitting tail coat made of fur, and in the Thule District it was so short it barely reached his hips where its trim of polar bear skin formed a seal with the hunter's bear skin trousers. Elsewhere in the Eskimo area trousers were made

wealth status was displayed. His labrets in a sense were his "badge" of rank, so too was the headband commonly worn and later the beads with which the Alaskan Eskimos decorated their clothing; but with rank came also a social obligation to be generous and charitable towards those who were less fortunate.

No matter how beautifully made a garment might be, it was only considered good if it was functional.

The Eskimos' passion for beads was carried to the extreme on the west coast of Greenland. What started as a simple bead choker about 300 years ago has now grown into a cape.

from sealskin or caribou, or simply not worn at all as in the case of the Aleut and Pacific Eskimos whose extra long parka made them superfluous.

On the whole there were comparatively few adornments or decorations. There was some skin mosaic work, some fringing and embroidery, all beautifully worked and in perfect taste, but rarely was such work seen in the days when clothing was considered good only if it was functional. Nevertheless, the Eskimos had their fashion absurdities and the most obvious of these was the gape of flesh, Even to this day it is impossible for a Thule woman wearing blue-and-silver foxskin "hot pants" and the long white sealskin boots to bend over without flashing at least four inches of naked thigh, or for a Polar Eskimo hunter

to squat without exposing a few pale inches of leg. They had designed each item to meet its neighbour with an interlock of fur and not to overlap and, as a result, any bending, twisting or stretching bursts the whole outfit open along these annular lines of weakness as though the furry monster had been slashed by an unseen sword. Their answer to this was to carry several fox tails with them when they went on a long journey and these they would tie around their legs to protect the naked part or stuff into the tops of the woman's thigh-length boots.

There has also developed in the last 100 years an uncontrolled passion for bead work among the women in Greenland, and what started out as a simple bead choker about 300 years ago when the

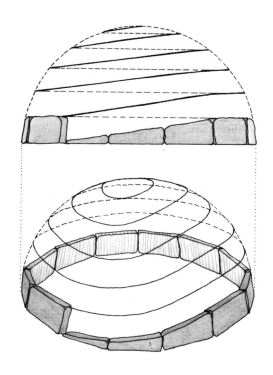

practice right across the Arctic; but only in Alaska and the Aleutian Islands did the men indulge in the barbaric splendour of decorating their faces with labrets of stone or ivory in the corners of the mouth and painting themselves on ceremonial occasions. Among most tribes the house dress was nothing more than a diaper of skin, for their stone dens were stifling and they could build up a pretty good heat even in the igloo, which may come as a surprise to anyone who is unfamiliar with the principles behind this, the most maligned of all Eskimo inventions.

Sheltering from the storm

For the past 400 years the igloo has been a popular theme for the scurrilous comedian and the peddler of

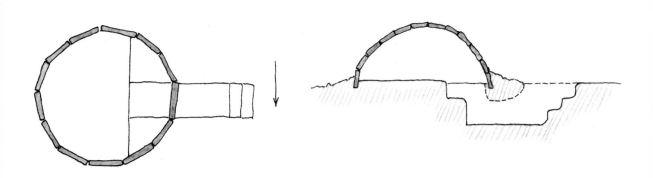

The most maligned of all Eskimo inventions is the igloo, and yet this dome of snow blocks was a structural discovery which antedated the Roman arch and the domes of the Moslem masons by at least 4,000 years.

whalers bartered beads for skins, ended up as a garish "chain mail" cape of beads which extends almost to the elbows. This, together with several other beautifully worked but totally impractical items of clothing, is now the national dress. In the old days a woman's only concession to vanity was her tattoo, and facial tattooing was common

jokes. For some inexplicable reason it even strikes the sophisticated mind as absurd if not pathetic. And when combined with the popular image of the Eskimo as a furry, slit-eyed, smiling dwarf crawling out of a tunnel of snow on all fours like a dog, the very suggestion that this dome of snow blocks was a structural invention which ante-

dates the Roman arch and the domes of the Moslem masons by at least 4,000 years is seen as laughable. And yet this is a fact, and to see an igloo nearing completion is breathtaking proof that the Eskimo at one stage in his history was way in advance of all other races on Earth. True, a block of snow is easier to handle than a block of stone, for each block of snow can be shaved with a knife to fit the one on which it is sitting and the one against which it is leaning; but to build in a spiral with each tier leaning inwards at a greater angle than the tier below, until only the key block remains to be shaved and set carefully in place at the top of the dome leaves me without the slightest doubt that its inventor was a genius.

Nor did he concentrate his genius only on the dome, for having built his shelter he had then to solve the problem of how to keep it warm. Essentially this was a problem of thermodynamics: if he made an

entrance hole in the igloo wall, the warm air of the interior, being lighter than the cold outside air, would escape through the upper half of the doorway as the cold air flowed in at ground level. By building a long entrance passage and hanging a skin curtain at the entrance he partially solved the problem; but then he had the brilliant

Brilliant though the invention was, it had two limitations: its size of course was the first of these, its sensitivity to heat the other.

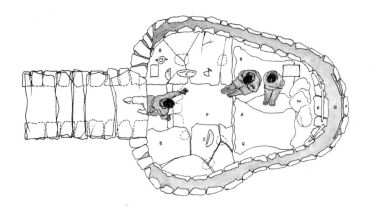

Above: Thule Eskimo's winter house. A: sleeping platform; B: side bench; C: stone blubber lamp; D: flag-stone floor: E: inside foundation stones; F: outside foundation stones; G: turf; H: skin lining; I: entrance door; J: meat (thawing out; K: Cooking pot; L: gut-skin window; M: clothing; N: roof beams (driftwood); O: ventilation hole: P: floor well; Q: entrance tunnel; R: skins.

Above right: for 5,000 years the design of the stone and turf den remained unaltered.

idea of tunnelling under the igloo and surfacing in a cold trap or pit in front of the sleeping platform. In this way he could leave his door open and the cold air would come in, fill the pit but rise no higher than the base of the sleeping platform as long as the igloo was heated. He made a small vent at the top of the dome to allow foul air to escape and create a healthy circulation of air, and he made a window in the wall of the igloo above the entrance tunnel with a sheet of freshwater ice.

His next move was to glaze the interior by raising the temperature until the snow began to thaw, and when the whole of the interior was thoroughly wet he would turn off the heat and allow the water to freeze. This glaze of ice gave the dome great strength and had the added advantage that a man could

rub against the walls without bringing down a shower of snow crystals which would thaw out and wet the caribou skins that covered the sleeping platform.

The igloo was now ready for occupation and its interior temperature could be regulated by neutralizing it with that of the outside air at the interface which formed the walls of his shelter. If the heat from his stove started melting the dome, he would go outside, climb up on the dome and shave off a few inches of snow. If he could not get the igloo warm enough he would shovel some more snow on. There was no fear of the igloo collapsing under his weight when he was doing these jobs, for once it had been glazed it was strong enough to support even a polar bear—which was just as well for occasionally it had to! It is also

Now the Eskimos live in villages like this one on Herbert Island in north-west Greenland, or in the larger settlements and towns. Even the Polar Eskimos who travel in the dead of winter prefer to carry a lightweight tent and fuel for their primus and pressure lamp rather than build an igloo—for in this way they can not only camp where they please, but they can camp at least 16 kilometres (10 miles) further on or feel warm at least two hours earlier.

worth mentioning that he could raise the inside temperature still higher without risk of melting the snow dome by lining the igloo with skins suspended from strings frozen into the walls, and could join several igloos together to form a hamlet which from the outside looked like a rash of blisters. But the snow house, however skilfully

In order to reduce the hunting pressure on the game around the larger settlements, the Canadian Government in 1953 encouraged six families from Port Harrison and Pond Inlet to move north to the uninhabited south coast of Ellesmere Island. The experiment, however, was slow in taking root for the two groups were culturally incompatible, and it was not until 1964 when they were physically united in a row of almost identical houses that they began to accept their new identity as the people of Grise Fjord.

it was made and maintained, had its limitations, for it could only be built with wind-packed snow and used when the air temperature was well below freezing.

Quite apart from these practical considerations there were also many cultural variations in the design and use of the igloo. In the region around Coronation Gulf where the Eskimos lived in snow houses right through the winter, this form of shelter, as one would expect, was structurally close to perfection. Elsewhere the craft of the snow mason was less well developed; in southern Alaska the techniques were unknown, for here and in other parts of the Arctic where there was no scarcity of wood or whale bone or where stone and turf was readily to hand, the Eskimos had applied their inventive skills to solving different structural problems with results that were just as impressive.

The ground plan of these more solid structures varied from place to place, but the general principle was much the same: a low wall of turf and stone slabs was built up around a shallow pit dug out of the frozen soil, and this wall supported beams of timber or the jaw bone and ribs of a whale which in turn supported a roof of sods. Then there was the Eskimos' cantilever system of spanning a gap—another brilliant discovery which was thousands of years in advance of the Europeans. By placing large slabs of stone on a low wall so that the slab projected on both sides of it like a capital letter "T", additional slabs could be laid on the inside to form the roof providing they were carefully counter-balanced with weights on the outside ledge.

In both of these buildings the long entrance passage sloped upwards towards the house and opened into

the den in the same sort of cold trap found in the igloo; similarly the sleeping platform was raised above the level of the entrance. But the effluvia of sweating bodies, rotten meat and stale urine which they kept for curing skins and washing their hair—smells which effectively formed a barrier in the entrance tunnel to most of the early European explorers who were curious to see what the den was like—bothered even the Eskimos in the summer. So it was the practice of these people to open the roof to give the hut an airing, and move into tents made of skins when the smells were at their worst.

It is also significant that when there was several years accumulation of bones and blubber outside the entrance of the den and this hill of yellow grease was even threatening to seal them in, it would never occur to the Eskimo to clear it up for with a little more effort and a lot more enthusiasm he could build another house!

The social and cultural differences between the groups who live at Grise Fjord, however, are still a bone of contention, for the Eskimos are great believers in methods —each group arguing that their way of doing things must be right for how else would their tribe have survived.

There is the same fierce conviction among the Polar Eskimos that their techniques of hunting and travelling are superior to all others but today, impressed by what they have seen at Grise Fjord, the Polar Eskimos are weighing up the pros and cons of replacing their dogs with snowmobiles. The people from Grise Fjord on the other hand tend to envy the Greenlanders their unregimented villages and their more traditional way of life.

85

CHAPTER SEVEN

THE TECHNIQUE OF SURVIVAL

It is most unlikely that the Eskimo ever had a *sudden* inspiration either to invent a new piece of equipment, or to refine a proven one—and the same we may assume applies to his techniques. Nor can we credit the Eskimo with having a head start on the Neolithic hunting cultures of northern Europe, for intelligent though he was, it would seem it took him at least 6,000 years to adapt to life on the arctic coast.

As hunters they had spread out and by about 4,600 years ago some of them had reached north-east Greenland, which is a long haul from Alaska for a people who had not yet learned to make use of the dog. Whether they dragged their cargo over the snow on skins or carried it we do not know; but there is certainly no archaeological evidence to suggest that they had the dog much before 3,800 years ago, and not until the Okvik culture came on the scene about 2,260 years ago did the Eskimos have anything that remotely resembled a sledge. It was much the same with the rest of his gear—his harpoons, lances, darts and boats—all took a very long time to mature to the point at which further refinement seemed either unnecessary or just plain impossible.

The sledge and the dog

In its original form the sledge was nothing more sophisticated than a pair of timber runners curved up at the front and held apart and parallel to each other by several cross-slats of wood. On this platform of cross-slats the cargo was carried about twenty centimetres (eight inches) or so above the surface on which the runners slid, and the whole structure was held together by thongs of skin so that the lashings "worked" when the sledge was being hauled over ice hummocks and ridges or along the skirt of frozen spray that encrusted the rocky coast. But from whom did the Eskimo get the idea? Not from his neighbour the Indian whose toboggan was like a flat-bottomed boat, for suitable though the toboggan was for the deep soft snow of the boreal forests, it was useless to the Eskimo. And so we must credit him with having invented the *komatik*, and marvel at his ingenuity, for when he had no wood to hand, he made his runners from rolled-up frozen muskox skins or from his catch of fish!

Driftwood is plentiful enough along some stretches of the arctic coast, but in other parts it is not—it depends on the direction of the currents rather than on the proximity of some great river which is spewing out its load of logs, uprooted trees and flotsam into the Arctic Ocean. All along the east and south-west coasts of Greenland there

The Polar Eskimo is a long-range hunter. He seldom travels with his dogs less than 5,000 kilometres (3,000 miles) a year and without question is the most self-sufficient traveller the world has ever seen.

In Canada and Alaska the machine has taken the place of the dog team and few hunters regret this, for the dog was slow and had a mind of its own. The Polar Eskimos on the other hand, who run large teams of dogs and can use them for up to eight months of the year, have yet to be convinced that the machine could serve them better. Occasionally they have to use their dogs to haul their sledges along the coast over tundra and naked rock. This the snowmobile could not do, nor does a machine have the tremendous range of a well-trained team of dogs.

The dog team is not only a transport system—it is a part of their way of life.

is driftwood to be found that is 8,000-odd kilometres (5,000 miles) "downstream" from the Russian rivers Ob, Yenisey and Lena. The Canadian Mackenzie brings down enormous quantities of wood which the currents scatter and sooner or later dump upon the beaches of the western arctic coast. But in the region around the North Magnetic Pole the currents deliver nothing in the summer except a load of winter ice, and it was not uncommon for the Eskimos from there to travel many hundreds of miles in search of men or beaches that had a supply of wood.

For this prized material an Eskimo might even kill, and certainly no man from the woodless regions had the slightest compunction about bartering a fractious

wife for a straight-grained length of pine or spruce. Not only was wood the best material from which to make the shafts of his harpoons and leisters, the frame and paddle of his *kayak* and the runners of his sledge, but any one of these items had a higher value than a woman among the Central tribes however good natured and industrious she was. Much to the chagrin of the hunter's wife, so also had a man's dogs.

Where there was food enough to feed a few dogs and a plentiful supply of wood the women had a better deal; but there were few hunting grounds that were rich enough to support large teams of dogs. On Herbert Island in the Thule District of north-west Greenland, that small community of 11 hunters with whom for two years I travelled and hunted had to kill, gut, bring home and store, thaw out, cut up and distribute a total of 74 tons of meat a year in order to feed the 150 ravenous animals they used for hauling their sledges. In terms of living flesh and bone this could amount to as many as 1,100 seals or 82 bull walruses a year, so it is hardly surprising that in past times the dogs were always the first to go hungry when a hunting com-

The Eskimo's "range" depends on the strength and stamina of his dogs and the nature of the country across which he is travelling. If his load is light and his dogs are many and he takes the trouble to ice the runners of his sledge every few hours of his journey, he can average 80 kilometres (50 miles) a day and still leave time to hunt for food along the way.

munity ran short of luck or a slight change of climate affected the distribution of game.

But the quantity, variety and consistency of a hunting community's harvest of meat did not only have a direct bearing on the quality of the dogs—it affected every aspect of Eskimo culture, for where there was an abundance of food a community had the time it needed to refine its equipment and to experiment with new techniques; whereas in the poorer regions, all this creative energy and skill was consumed by the hunter's continual struggle to keep himself and his family alive.

The harpoon and float

Like the sledge, the harpoon was common throughout the Eskimo area and yet its design and quality varied according to the ingenuity and "pride" of the individual groups, even though in its essentials it was everywhere the same.

The head was made of walrus ivory or caribou antler, inset with a blade of flint or bone, and to this head was attached a sealskin line which held it in place at the top of the foreshaft by friction within the socket of the head and tension on the thong. This foreshaft, which was seldom more than fifteen centimetres (six inches) long, was also of ivory and was tied to the mainshaft in such a way that the foreshaft acted like a double-jointed finger and the thongs as its ligaments. The mainshaft of the harpoon was made of wood or of several pieces of bone lashed to-

harpoon having delivered its sting had twisted clear, but it could not drift away because the line between the hunter and his quarry passed through a loop of sealskin which was, along with a few other "refinements", lashed securely to the shaft.

What happened then would to some extent depend on the quarry. Generally speaking, the bigger it was the more difficult and dangerous the struggle became. But the setting, the animal and the whole development of the hunt from the first sighting to the kill were different every time, and it was in this unpredictable element that the real danger lay.

Hunting the walrus in the dark from a thin and flexible platform of ice at the very edge of a "smoking" sea was one of the greatest tests of skill. Here the hunter had only the friction of his harpoon line around a lance which he had hastily driven into the ice on which to hold well over a ton of heaving fury—and without a doubt, the walrus is the most fearless and powerful of all the animals that live in the arctic sea. I have seen a walrus smash its head through twenty centimetres (eight inches) of ice several times in the space of three minutes in an effort to get at its tormentors and tear them to pieces with its tusks. This was the unpredictable element of that particular hunt and one of the longest three minutes I have ever spent in my life, for the ice was covered by a crust of rime and the slightest movement on our part would almost certainly have been our last, so there was nothing else we could do but hold our breath while the walrus punched holes in the ice all around us until finally it surfaced three metres (ten feet) away and my Eskimo companion got his shot.

An incident such as that in the

gether so that the whole thing when "set" was a well-balanced projectile exactly the height of its owner; but unlike the spear or the lance which essentially were stabbing weapons and had therefore to be all in one piece, the harpoon was an ingenious device which on the shock of impact "broke" into its three separate parts.

Its function, as you have probably guessed, was not to kill, but to attach an animal to a line at the other end of which was a hunter, and for this to be effective the harpoon head had to penetrate the body of the animal to a depth of at least ten centimetres (four inches). Only then would the tug on the line turn the head sideways in the wound and anchor itself in the flesh. Meanwhile, the shaft and foreshaft of the days before the gun would have been even more hazardous, for the aboriginal hunter had only the lance and the knife. Hunting from an open lead in the polar pack was very much safer for there the hunter had a firmer footing. He also had a more effective and safer way of granted the process of thought behind the invention. But the mind of the Eskimo did not work by logical progression. He took his clues from the world about him and never strayed off into theory when there was an alternative route through fact. His equipment re-

tiring a whale or a walrus he had harpooned from an open boat: he would take the skin from a seal by rolling it back in much the same way you peel off a sock, and after stitching up the openings at each end, he would blow it up and insert a plug. The result was something resembling a seal that was about to burst, and with this bladder of air attached to the line, its buoyancy not only acted as a drag on the diving whale, but also as a marker float which from time to time would reappear as the tiring whale came up to breathe. All that remained for the hunter to do was to stay in the vicinity of the float and wait for an opportunity to get in close for the kill.

It all seems so simple and obvious that we tend to take for flected this; so too did his techniques. Clothing apart, you won't find an artefact dating from any stage of his cultural development over the last 8,000 years that was not perfectly functional, or a hunting method that was not based on a profound understanding of the nature and the anatomy of his prey. It was a foolproof survival system in which innovation was regarded as an unnecessary risk, and although in effect this restricted his progress on an intellectual level, it improved his equipment and technique, for it concentrated all his creative energy on refining the proven system. The *kayak* is a good example.

The boat of skin and bone

In the chain of food where so many

Later in the year and from the edge of an open lead in the pack ice the walrus is easy game. For the long-range hunter and his dogs it provides a rare chance to eat their fill.

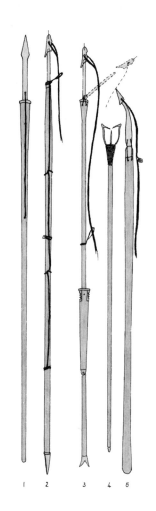

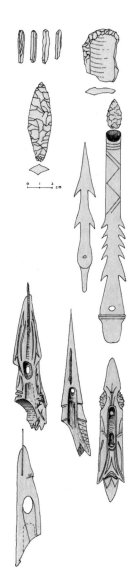

Eskimo hunting implements. Left: 1. lance; 2. ice hunting harpoon with fixed foreshaft and harpoon line held in the hand; 3. kayak harpoon with jointed foreshaft and harpoon line attached to sealskin bladder — note also the throwing-stick; 4. salmon spear or leister; 5. whale harpoon with jointed foreshaft, line attached to sealskin bladder.
Top right: micro-blades, scrapers and projectile points from the campus site near Fairbanks, Alaska. Dated 6400 BC.
Right: ivory harpoon heads of the Okvik, Ipiutak and Old Bering Sea Cultures and pronged harpoon heads of the Palaeo-Aleuts 4,000 years ago.

animals that were competing with him were either faster or a good deal stronger, the Eskimo's only hope of survival lay in directing all his talents on the weakness of his quarry. Now this presented the Eskimo with no great problem as far as the land animals were concerned for these he could catch with snares, traps, nets or tricks of one sort or another; but those whose natural element was the sea were a tougher proposition. To get on terms with them he needed a boat — a one-man floating armoury that could skid across the sea so arrow-straight and silently that no surface target had the time or the power to get out of its way. By about the year 2000 BC the Palaeo-Aleuts had made a boat from skin and bone which for its size was already without equal in speed or grace, in weight, simplicity or style. And by the time the Eskimo entered the literature of the Western World towards the end of the sixteenth century, its design and the techniques of using it were impossible to improve upon.

Naturally this had greatly impressed the early explorers, and some had even gone to the trouble of measuring the *kayak* in the hope of discovering the secret of its speed; but no amount of measuring can describe a work of art, for the harmony of shape and line which is so pleasing to the eye is in its structure as a whole. These early explorers had in any case failed to realize that all the measurements take on a new relationship when the boat and man are one. On its own, this long sleek craft is without a single vertical to justify its length, and beautiful though it is to behold, the boat is cold and dead. But put boat and man together and something magical occurs: suddenly the boat becomes the seated extension of the man and he its dynamic, its soul, its very reason for existence— what's more, its length is exactly

By early summer when the walrus herds come out on to the ice to bathe in the warmth of the sun, the Eskimo does not need to kill them for there are plenty of seals around that are doing the same thing.

Sometimes when the sea is like glass and the hunter has been waiting for hours, motionless and mesmerized and soaking up the sun, he will have the strange sensation that he is floating not upon the sea but in the air between two worlds each of which is the undistorted image of the other. Not even the steamy snorts of a school of whales or the soft splash of a nearby seal will set him free and should he capsize while he is under the spell he will almost certainly drown.

Because of the risk of falling into a trance the kayak hunters usually preferred to hunt in pairs or even in small flotillas when the sea was calm. In Alaska, however, with three men in a boat, this was never a problem.

three times his height and all the ratios between boat and man make sound mathematical sense. And how are we to account for this?

Either the Eskimo had a flair for mathematics at least equal to that of the Megalithic "astronomers" of Britain and France who were his Stone Age contemporaries, or he was a man of artistic genius, and it seems pretty obvious to me that since he had neither the "logical" approach nor fingers and toes enough on his body to count in

In Greenland over the last hundred years the umiak has been used primarily as a cargo boat.

excess of twenty without borrowing another man, the *kayak* must have been an artist's boat and those mathematically exact proportions based simply on the aesthetic principle that what looked right *was* right.

But the joy he derived from making a *kayak* was nothing compared to the pure delight he got out of using it. With the hem of his waterproof anorak tied tightly around the coaming of the *kayak* and around his wrists and face he felt united with the sea. If he capsized he could right himself by a skilful movement of his paddle, or if this was lost, he could use his harpoon, and some men, their hands alone. All his gear: the harpoon, line, lance and knife and the sealskin bladder or *avataq* were carried on deck under thongs of skin. On the west coast of Greenland where the *kayak* was used mainly for hunting seals, a special stand on which the harpoon line lay coiled sat lashed to the foredeck within arm's reach, and midway between the stand and the bow a white screen

was set square rigged like a sail.

All hunters these days of course use the gun and this is carried in a sheath of canvas or skin directly in front of him, while his spare sweater and socks, his primus stove and the waterproof bag in which he carries his tea, sugar and hard tack biscuits are stuffed into the tiny space just behind the seat. Thus equipped he can paddle away alone or with a flotilla of friends, and never is he in closer communion with the spirits of his past than when he is mirrored in a glass-like sea with nothing else to do but wait and meditate, soak up the sensual warmth of the sun— and after a while, move on.

Hunting from the larger skin boat was a totally different experience, for whereas with the *kayak* the solitary hunter could slip silently into the wake of a passing narwhal and with a sudden burst of speed overhaul and harpoon it, the *umiak* was an unwieldy craft, six to nine metres (twenty to thirty feet) in length which positively bulged with men and bristled with their weapons.

In Alaska on the other hand the umiak *was, and still is, used mainly for whaling.*

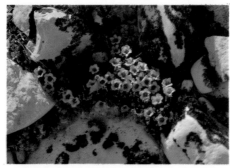

Plants are better adapted to the rigorous conditions of the Arctic than the animals that live in the North. Whereas a frozen animal will die, a frozen plant will simply lie dormant throughout the winter and, if necessary, remain so for hundreds or even thousands of years while it waits for the return of warmth, light and moisture to reawaken it and start the sap coursing through its cells. Without this special ability which is unique among all forms of life on earth, the Arctic would be barren and unable to support a single animal, bird or insect which are all part of that chain of food that begins and ends with the plant.

In fact it took a crew of eight and they even had a skipper, although to be more correct, the *umialik* or boat owner actually "owned" a crew. The relationship was essentially an economic one. He bid for their services on the open market or bribed them to break loyalty with another boat and join him. Having formed his crew, he had not only to keep them in clothing and equipment, but he had to offset any rival bids by offering his men all manner of gratuities to keep himself in business. And "business" is about the only word to describe the whaling system as it developed in Alaska.

His profit was what was left of the whale after it had been divided, but since one large whale could weigh as much as sixty tons, he needed to share only one of these a year with another skipper in order to break even, and if his boat took a whale unaided, he had ample reserves of meat with which to trade for goods with the inland tribes, and these goods he passed on to his men or used as bribes to attract more skilful hunters from other crews to join him.

The prestige that went with the title *umialik* was of course enormous, and so too was his wealth when the whales obliged him; but this, as I have said before, they would do only if all the rituals and sanctions had been scrupulously observed, and so complex was the cult of the whale and so uncompromising were the conditions, it may seem a little surprising that the hunters caught any at all.

It may seem even more surprising, considering the distrust of the Eskimo for any form of authority, that this communal form of hunting lasted right through to the present day—a span of at least 4,000 years in some parts of Alaska. True, there was no other way to kill a huge whale than to go out and meet it with a team of men and a boatload of harpoons and floats. But this is not the whole answer, for part of it lies in the paradox that individuality cannot be expressed except through a close relationship with others. Of course, socially the Eskimo *was* cooperative and the *umialik* was no exception. And as for that constant tug of war between his religion and his skill—skill invariably won hands down, but this was never admitted for fear of offending the gods.

The hunters' stratagem

In the Arctic the yearly cycle in the life of every plant and creature with the exception of man is an imprecise measure of time which begins when the sun's warmth melts the snow and softens the frozen ground. It is then, as their roots feed on the nutrients and the moisture in the soil and their leaves soak up the energy of the low-circling arctic sun that the dormant plants stir from their sleep and begin to swell and throb. It is then that the birds flock back to the North with a fevered urge to mate and nest, and the female bear at last leaves the lair in which she had kept her bear cubs warm and once again goes on the prowl. The ringed seals are giving birth to their pups in the slippery snow caves in the ice; the white whales too are calving now and so are the harp seals further south. And while the great whales on their migration north towards their summer feeding grounds are cruising into Baffin Bay and through the Bering Strait, the caribou are swarming from the forests to the sea.

But the Eskimo, glad though he is to see the sun and its effect on the world around him, is under no compulsion to procreate in spring and therefore remains immune from that infectious sense of urgency which seems to have taken possession of every living thing. For him, one season drifts into another and there is no point at which they begin. Nor is there any significance for him in the division of time into units called days or any advantage to be gained through the knowledge of how many of these irrelevant units go to make a year. Where then are we to begin? Where else than at that moment in time when the sea on which he had been boating, overnight becomes a surface upon which the hunter can walk.

No event in the yearly cycle of the Eskimo is more dramatic than this, nor is there a single event which gives him greater joy. Within a few hours of the sea freezing over, the hunters are out on the smooth ice sliding along on sandals of bear skin with a harpoon in one hand and a lance in the other heading for the sounds of a snorting seal. Risky though it is, the sense of freedom the hunter feels is indescribable and no other stratagem of hunting is easier than this—he skates towards his quarry in long sliding strides whenever he hears it breathing, and stands motionless when it dives until eventually he is standing poised over the hole with his harpoon held almost vertically waiting for the seal to surface.

But this is a short-lived technique, for with the first fall of snow it is no longer possible to approach the seal without making a sound, and the slightest sound will frighten it away. From then on until the following spring when the seals will come out on to the ice to bask in the warmth

Spring in the High Arctic is the month of June. This is the month when the sun spirals up to its highest point and Nature is suddenly driven frantic with the urge to procreate. The Eskimo, however, being a practical man, is not caught up in this seasonal rush to reproduce, but turns it to his advantage by feasting on the fat female eider ducks and their delicious eggs.

The Angmagssalik hunter, Kuitse (photographed in 1906) was a great hunter with polar bear scars to prove how close he had come to death.

The shooting screen commonly used in Greenland is a far more elaborate piece of equipment than that used elsewhere in the Arctic, but the principle is the same: the hunter hides behind the screen when the seal is on the lookout and creeps towards his quarry only during the fifteen to twenty seconds in which it is asleep.

of the sun, the hunter must use a technique which requires a good deal more patience than skill.

Even finding a seal's breathing hole is difficult enough for it may be no more than an inch in diameter and the only indication that a hole is there is the slight mound of rime which forms around the hole when the seal comes up to breathe. A dog will find it easily enough if the scent is fresh, but it must first be guided to a likely spot, and having found it, the dog must be tethered far enough away so as not to disturb the quarry. The hunter then prepares the hole: he first removes the snow covering the hole and probes the cavity in the ice with a curved stick or antler so that he knows exactly the angle at which the seal will enter. He then carefully covers the hole with snow and places an "indicator" in the hole—something that will give him a warning signal that the seal has entered and is in the right position for the kill. Then comes the wait.

Sometimes many hours may pass without any sign of activity in the hole, for every seal keeps several holes open, and throughout this long wait the hunter must not make a sound or let his attention wander from the sliver of bone or whatever he is using as an indicator. This is a good opportunity for the hunter's son to get in some practice at driving dogs, for by driving around some distance from the hole at which his father is waiting he can delude the seal into believing that the only safe hole is the one at which there is no sound.

A net weighted to hang vertically under the ice like a curtain near a breathing hole is a very much easier way of catching seals. Surprisingly this method is unknown in the Central region, where they developed an alternative method of hunting with the harpoon whereby two men worked together. The technique, which is used by very few hunters these days, is to have two holes in the sea ice within an arm's reach of each other; at the one stands a man with a long harpoon, at the other his partner lies peering into the hole with his head and the hole covered over so that he has a clear view down into the sea. The prone hunter guides the harpoon with one hand, and by whistling and moving the harpoon up and down creates a vibration at the head of the harpoon where two small pieces of bone are fastened. Needless to say, the seal is driven out of its mind with curiosity and when it is directly under the harpoon the standing hunter thrusts it down into the seal's body.

The netting method of course has some disadvantages, otherwise you may be sure the Eskimos would have used nothing else. For one thing, the nets have to be laid within a few days of the sea ice forming and before the seals have established a regular set of breathing holes, so there is always a chance that the position might prove unproductive, and even supposing the net has been ideally placed, say beneath a tidal crack in the ice along the coast, pressure might close the crack or it may open so wide that it will tear the nets to shreds. But the great advantage of the nets as far as the Polar Eskimos are concerned is that they can with luck provide a supply of fresh meat through the two-month period when it is too dark to use the harpoon. They are also an occasional provider of fresh meat for the family while the hunter is away on his long spring journeys. These, among the Polar Eskimos, are seldom less than 1,600 kilometres (1,000 miles), for their hunting territory covers a radius of at least 500 kilometres (300 miles) in which they know every stretch of coastline, every pass, valley and glacier like the back of their hands.

The purpose of these journeys is to hunt the bear, but not for the reason one might first suppose, for although they need the polar bear's pelt, there is a need much more important than this which drives the Eskimos on—a need which only became clear to me the first time I shared the experience with them. Suddenly I realized that hunting the polar bear is quite unlike any other hunt, at least for the Eskimo, for there in the middle of Smith Sound there was space, speed, skill and blind courage combining in a drama which was plunging headlong into a savage poetry of conflict that had all begun with the first excited whisper . . . "Nanoooo!" and the pointing of a finger.

The cargo lashings had been slashed with a knife and the whole

There is no standard technique for catching the white whale or beluga. It is hunted from the ice floes, from the kayak and sometimes even a motor boat; but whatever the method, without a good deal of luck and a split-second reaction from the hunter when he sees his chance, this whale would rarely be taken. This picture shows part of a catch of no less than eight belugas—all of them killed by one man who had the luck and the skill to back it up.

load dumped on the ice to lighten the sledge, and within a matter of seconds it was scorching the ice behind thirteen dogs at full gallop straight for the bear. The hunter had crawled along the sledge, hauled in the dogs' traces hand over hand, and selecting three from the fan of traces that led to his best bear dogs, he had them cut loose. Off they had gone at an incredible speed after the bear which by now was in full flight towards the nearest stretch of open water while the sledge thundered on after them. The hunter released more and more dogs to join those that were now circling the bear, diving at its flanks and leaping on to its back. Some were being swept off the bear, others were being knocked flying through the air; some were slashed open and bleeding, the skull of one dog had been crushed with one blow of the bear's massive paw. The noise, the animal odours of blood and fear, the climax as the hunter hit his target and the bear crumpled into the mass of yapping dogs—all of this action: the drama of the chase, the kill, the pride of the hunter in his dogs, his sorrow at the one he had lost—it all amounted to one thing: that he needed the bear not as a predator needs its prey, but as a challenge through which to reaffirm his own ability.

All the animals he hunts are a test of his skill and a few a test of his courage; but only with the solitary, wandering bear, does the Eskimo have an affinity. It is, they say, the only animal whose courage and cunning is the equal of man and for this reason they admire him. Indeed, some tribes are even in awe of the bear and until quite recently, the greatest hunters, out of respect for its noble spirit, would not think of killing a bear with a gun, but

Bird netting is a skill which is soon mastered for the little auks return to the steep rocky slopes of their breeding ground at certain times of the day in swarms of hundreds of thousands.

Fishing with nets requires practically no skill at all. There is therefore a tendency among the keen young hunters to feel themselves a cut above these two simple but delightful summer activities — which of course suits the old folk and the children very well.

instead would use a lance, and the bravest among them nothing more than a knife. But essential though the bear is in feeding the ego of the hunter, the seal is his staff of life, and as summer approaches and the seals come out on to the ice, a few of the best hunters will put to the test a traditional skill which is fast dying out—that of approaching their timorous quarry to within a few feet by dressing in sealskin and aping its movements so cleverly that the short-sighted seal suspects nothing, until, of course, it is too late and its companion has transformed himself into a man and slit its throat with a knife.

It is the combination of the target standing out clearly against a white background and the deadly accuracy of the marksman that has all but ousted this technique. But the rifle has replaced the lance and the bow and arrow, not the harpoon; nor has it in every case reversed the order in which they are used. A narwhal will sink like a stone when it is shot, so will the white whale and the ringed seal late on in the summer, and the only way to be sure of the capture is to get the harpoon into the quarry first and use the rifle later. Of course, there are no golden rules that will cover every type of game: the hunter, for example, will often aim to miss a seal—to merely frighten it into a dive before it has had a chance to take a deep breath; it will not, therefore, be able to stay down for so long or be able to swim far from where the hunter last saw it. In this way the hunter can get in close enough to a breathless seal to be certain of a head shot and to get his harpoon in before the seal starts sinking. Even so, the hunter needs the capability of a long throw,

and seated in a craft in which balance is so critical, the long throw is not possible without two refinements to the harpoon. One of these is a pair of flat wings of bone inset at the butt of the shaft; the other is the throwing board which, acting as an extension of his arm, increases the force of his throw considerably. It is unlikely, however, that these two refinements were his invention, for similar spear-throwers have been found in many parts of the world.

A more sedate occupation by comparison is the caribou hunt in the autumn when the caribou are in good coat and moving towards their regular crossing places along certain rivers in the Canadian Arctic. The Eskimos here in the old days would wait for them and when the herd was in midstream would go after them in their *kayaks*. In the water they were easy targets for lances; but on land they were a good deal more difficult to approach. The technique here was to build two converging rows of stone cairns to look like men, and funnel the animals towards the spot where the hunters with their bows and arrows were lying in wait. In those days the hunter had to be closer than twenty paces to hit his target— these days with high-powered rifles and telescopic sights and with fewer caribou on the move, much of the tension and the drama of this military-style ambush has been lost. It is much the same with the other land animals: the steel trap has replaced the ancient and often in- genious traps made from stones or driftwood, and only the fishing camps still have that timeless quality which links the Eskimo in Canada somewhat tenuously with his past.

CHAPTER EIGHT

THE WHITE
INVASION

It was 9,000 years after the Bering "bridge" had collapsed behind the Eskimos and separated the Old World from the New before the Vikings found their way on to the American Continent by a different route and returned to tell the tale; but they were not the first to make this perilous voyage—they were merely the first to prove beyond a shadow of doubt that they had done so.

There is, for instance, a mass of circumstantial evidence to suggest that the Irish monks in their search for the "Island of Promise" had made landings in the Caribbean, on the American mainland and on the south-west coast of Greenland sometime around about AD 570: their skin-covered curraghs were excellent sea-boats, each was skippered by a Saint, and none of their descriptions could possibly have been drawn except on a basis of fact.

In no way, however, does this detract from the Viking achievement, nor should the fact that the Vikings discovered Iceland, Greenland and the American Continent only as the providential result of having been blown off course, for what the Vikings did that the Irish monks had failed to do was to follow up their discoveries and colonize.

The Skraelings

It was from the Norsemen, not from the Irish monks, that the Vatican first heard about the New World and about traces of a primitive culture which had been found by Eric the Red when he was looking around for a suitable site for his first winter den in AD 982. It was from these same colonists that there later came reports of flesh and blood natives—"swarthy, evil-looking men" who were encountered by Thorfinn Karlsefni in south-east Labrador during his attempt in 1003–06 to set up a colony on the American mainland—in fact, one of the reasons why the Norsemen failed to get a foothold in America was because they were constantly under attack. At least in Greenland at that time they had the whole country to themselves.

But then there appears one revealing sentence in a manuscript called the *History of Norway*, the original of which probably dates back to sometime before 1300: "farther to the north" it states, "hunters have come across small people whom they call *Scraelinga*; when they are hit their wounds turn white and they do not bleed, but when they die there is no end to the bleeding." Maybe the Norsemen with one hand on the cross and the other on the sword hilt were by that time only

It is all too easy to lay the blame for the present state of Eskimo society on the first white men they met. But whichever way you apportion the blame you will be left with a residue of doubt about whether the Eskimo was forced by circumstances to accept the fateful changes in his way of life, or whether of his own free will he chose to abandon the ways of the past and take a chance on the new.

The Norsemen who had settled in south-west Greenland were suspicious and sometimes aggressive, and the early English explorers, in spite of their good intentions, did not endear themselves to the natives by capturing a few as "specimens". But initially it was fame, fortune and rivalry that motivated the search for the North-West Passage, not the urge to conquer. Parry's contacts with the Eskimos on his 1821–23 expedition (top) were amiable enough; and so, for the most part were Franklin's in 1819–22 (bottom).

half as dangerous as they were in the days when they worshipped Odin and Thor; but clearly they were still too short-tempered and distrustful to live in peace with this new wave of "primitive" immigrants from the North.

They did not in any case need the Eskimos at that time, for the Norse community was strong and vigorous and their supply lines to Iceland and Norway, though tenuous, were adequate for their survival as a colony until about 1350 when the climate began to change in favour of the natives and the supply lines to the Norsemen's beach-head on the coast of Greenland were severed by the Black Death in the far-off port of Bergen. A few ships got through to Greenland in the latter part of the fourteenth century, and some scholars believe that life dragged on

at the Eastern Settlement during the first half of the fifteenth. By then, however, the Norsemen's only chance of survival lay in adopting the ways and the techniques of the Eskimo, and this they could not do because they were too proud and too foolish to recognize that the Eskimo in that environment was inferior to none. And inferior to none the Eskimo remained for the next 600 years.

As for when and how the last Norsemen died, that's anybody's guess. There were occasional fights between the settlers and the Eskimos and at the best of times they regarded each other with suspicion; but according to an old Greenlandic legend, the last of the Norsemen had been massacred by the *qavdlunât*— the people who had come from the south. Whether these raiders were Basque or English we have no way of knowing for the Eskimos on seeing the fleet approaching had fled with the wives and children of the Norsemen deep into the fjords, and there, according to the legend, they had married and lived happily and multiplied in peace.

The short cut to Cathay

It was, of course, a long time before word reached the Vatican and the Nordic Court that this Christian foothold in the New World had finally been wiped out and that Greenland once again was in the hands of the heathen. The fate of the Greenland settlers, meanwhile, continued to play on the consciences of successive Popes and Kings, and haunted them even more after the incentive for reopening the Viking routes had been taken from them by the Basques, the Portuguese and Dutch—not to mention that strange assortment of "Elizabethans" who were obsessed by their conviction

One should bear in mind that the four nations who among them had divided up the $3\frac{1}{2}$ million square miles ($8\frac{1}{2}$ million square kilometres) of what was once the Eskimos' territory, had each sprung from different roots and had a heritage of different traditions. They had also acquired their arctic territory at different times and under different ways of dealing with the Eskimos for whom eventually they became responsible under International Law.

It might be argued that some of the more accomplished polar travellers like Leopold McClintock and Dr John Rae did much to allay the instinctive fear which the Eskimos had for the whites.

century sailors could have arrived at this idea. We must remember, however, that the world was thought to be smaller in those days, and that when it became known that Columbus's "Spice Island" was a barrier at least 20,000 kilometres (13,000 miles) in length, it made more sense to look for a passage around the north of the American Continent. Such a route, the English believed, would enable them to tap the fabulous wealth of Cathay.

And so began a search that waxed and waned with the moods and fortunes of a nation which, ironically, had outgrown her need for a North-West Passage even before a single ship had entered it through the Hudson Strait, for by 1610, the English had broken the Spanish and Portuguese monopoly of the southern seas and her trading ships had reached Cathay by way of the Cape of Good Hope.

Why then did the search for the North-West Passage drag on for the next 300 years? Fame, fortune, rivalry, the challenge of the unknown perhaps—all of these motives can be found in the sailors who went in

that the shortest and safest route to the riches of the East lay in sailing north-west!

Looking at a modern globe it is hard to see how these sixteenth-

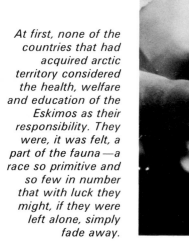

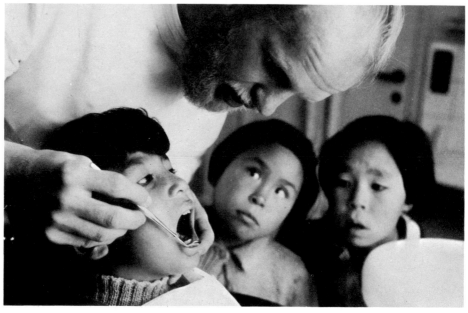

search of that short cut to Cathay; but none of them explain that fascination of the English with this particular route.

Time and again they returned to the problem, knowing full well that its solution would be of no practical use and that the gain of every small success was out of all proportion to the suffering and the sacrifice of human life. It was almost as though they had convinced themselves that there was some profound religious significance in the search for the North-West Passage—that the Creator had reserved His greatest rewards for those who ventured to the uttermost ends of the Earth.

The exploration and extension of British Arctic territory provided the Royal Navy with a foe in times of peace—a challenge which contrived not only to keep the cream of the navy occupied in a noble cause, but kept Britain supplied with heroes

In the wake of the explorers and occasionally in advance of them came the missionaries in droves to stake out territories for and on behalf of the Church each represented. The conversion of the heathen, so the missionaries believed, was for the heathen's good. The traders (left) of course were equally convinced that they were providing the primitive with the bare essentials a man required in order to survive.

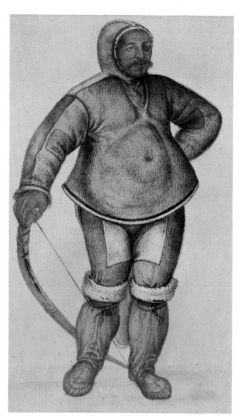
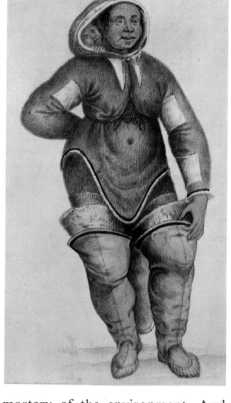

at a time when rampant patriotism and her ambition to influence the world was in constant need of living proof that she had what it takes to be great.

Not until the Franklin tragedy of 1845–48 and the shocking disclosure that some of these heroes had been reduced to cannibalism in their last desperate bid to stay alive, did the spotlight of public adoration shift from the naval prima donnas in the centre of the stage, to the lesser characters in the wings who in the course of scratching around for the remains of the ill-fated Franklin expedition had been quietly filling in the blanks on the map. These new heroes, however, were an entirely different breed of men. Loners most of them. Men with little or no regard for the gold braid of tradition, who in the course of living and travelling with the Eskimos were fast acquiring a

mastery of the environment. And with the last piece of the passage puzzle finally in place, they had set their sights on the Pole.

The sacrificial heathen

It was, of course, an entirely different set of rewards that had kept the commercial sponsors happy. In the wake of the explorers had come wave after wave of slaughterers, traders and ruthless exploiters in a white invasion totally lacking in principle or plan—a devastating flood of avaricious men who without compassion had plundered and ravaged the natural resources of the land and sea and ripped the delicate fabric of one of the finest primitive cultures the world has ever seen.

They in turn had been followed by the missionaries with their hunger for souls and their licence from a jealous God to destroy all competi-

Until as recently as 1945 the view was still held in some government circles that the primitive was best left to fend for himself. But then suddenly the whole Arctic seemed transformed overnight and, like some time-lapse film of nature, schools, hospitals, houses and flats, supermarkets, power-stations, factories and mines sprang up out of the frozen ground.

tion. Some, with a blind disregard for the dignity of man, had raped and tortured the primitive mind until their victims had screamed for mercy and renounced the whole philosophy upon which their way of life was based. It did not matter to the missionaries that they were crushing a culture which in its isolation and its ignorance of God had survived at least 6,000 years, for the conversion of the heathen, they believed, was for his own good.

But how could these missionaries in one breath preach the love of God and in the next condemn? Were they so bigoted that they could ignore that most humane of all civilized concepts—the concept of equality upon which the Christian Church was built? They not only could, they did. As far as the early missionaries were concerned, the Eskimos were an inferior race and no theological argument for the first 300 years of

In Greenland the change of pace which came at the end of the Second World War was less dramatic than in Canada and therefore less catastrophic. Under the benevolent rule of Denmark the Greenlanders had been moving slowly towards autonomy since the 1850s. By 1945 not only was practically the entire population literate, but they had already come through a social and cultural revolution during which they had abandoned their old way of life as hunters to become wage-earning fishermen.

Had the change from a hunting to a fishing economy been sudden the transformation of the Greenlanders' social culture would not have worked. But the Danes were not ad hoc innovators — they had carefully prepared their plan so that the transition was gradual, and one of the factors which helped ease the strain was the surplus supply of fish. This enabled the men to keep large teams of dogs with which they could go hunting or visiting during the winter months. Even the dogs of the unemployed could always find plenty of food around the quay and outside the fish storage sheds.

their reign was dug up to contradict them.

Occasionally some hint of these prejudices and frustrations came through in their written reports, as for instance the suggestion in 1724 by no lesser man than Hans Egede, the "Apostle of Greenland", that the heathen should be taxed in order to contribute something towards the cost of his own conversion! In his view the Eskimo was a "savage" and men of such "innate stupidity" needed not only correction and discipline, but needed to work for their salvation and if necessary would have to be "completely subjugated and made into slaves".

Clearly then, there could be no conversions by the conventional method of good example for the missionaries had neither the time nor any of the qualities which the aboriginal hunter admired in a man. His only hope of success, therefore, lay in first deriding the native beliefs and then generating fear with threats of eternal damnation in the

The Danes have based their development policy on the altruistic principle that a colonial power should seek not the enrichment of the ruler, but the advancement of the ruled, and since 1945 they have poured billions of dollars into various schemes which hopefully will form the basis of a viable economy. But in Alaska and the Canadian Arctic the Eskimos' problems are far greater for there has been no fishing industry to ease the shock of their transition into the 20th century. They have oil and minerals under their feet, but lacking the specialists' skills they cannot join the whites in exploiting these resources and at present, in spite of all the money that has been spent on their education, employment opportunities are mostly janitorial, unskilled and unsatisfactory.

fire of Hell for those who did not accept the Word or simply failed to understand what the Word was trying to say. For the trader to profit on the other hand, he had to undermine the system by encouraging aggression and the competitive spirit and exciting cravings for material wealth—all of which, needless to say, was as alien to the Eskimo as the concept of sin, and the selfishness, greed and envy which soon began to manifest itself as friction within the community.

So the missionaries believed they were saving souls, and the traders believed they were being of service by providing the primitive with the bare essentials which they considered a man required in order to survive.

Liquor and flour, guns, ammunition, tobacco and tea—all of these things came in with the white man, as did the diseases from which they died like flies.

For 200 years the tragic survivors of a once-proud race clung on to

the past while at the same time reaching out to the missionaries for help. It was a living nightmare unlike anything they had known before. But then suddenly, thirty-five years ago, the primitive was shaken awake by the noise of an army of construction workers building airstrips and military bases and soon all the areas of strategic importance became flooded with white men. The Eskimo got up and looked around and found that he was no longer free to wander about wherever he chose. He was herded along with the rest of his race into settlements where the whites had built schools and hospitals and houses of one sort for the natives and another for the white élite. He was now a captive animal dependent on his trainer for food, clothing, even the money for his booze, and as he lay in a corner sick at heart and weeping with savage self-contempt, he realized for the first time that what the white man said was true—he was inferior.

The Greenland Administration has its problems, for no one doubts that the standard of living has been artificially created by the enormous transfers of capital from the Danish Treasury, or that to maintain it, let alone improve it, the Danes will have to continue pouring in money. It is now clear that even with a considerable increase in productivity from the fisheries and mines, the province can never hope to pay its way. The whole policy is therefore under review, and even the Greenlanders themselves are arguing for a return to the more communal way of life and a standard of living which is determined by the Greenlanders themselves.

CHAPTER NINE

THE TRIBE THAT GOT AWAY

The Eskimo magician was sad. It had been fourteen years since the old man had been called upon to make the long and perilous flight to the moon to retrieve a stolen soul, and only twice in the past ten years had he been obliged to swim deep down into the silent world in search of *Arnaquagssâq—the* peevish old woman who ruled over the creatures of the sea. And perhaps it was just as well, for such journeys took a lot out of a man, and what little strength he had left he had needed over the last few years to support his reputation and dignity against the insidious influence of the missionaries upon the natives of his tribe.

Their acid condemnation of everything in which the Eskimos believed had already eaten into the very structure of the society. They had denounced as immoral a whole way of life, proclaiming as sinful anything they would not piously condone within their own close circle of narrow-minded friends. In place of a functional philosophy that had survived the test of 5,000 years, they offered their own Christian faith which to the untrained mind was totally unintelligible, and a set of commandments that was as irrelevant to a Polar Eskimo as his own taboos would have been to the tribes of Moses. But most of all they hated the old man, for he was an *angákoq*—an agent of the devil; devious, dangerous and, since he could not be converted, the sooner dead the better.

It is sad really, for the old man's life had been one of total devotion to the well-being of his people, and anyone but a missionary would have seen that. What he had seen and felt was to him the truth, and it hurt him deeply to be called a liar by the newly converted and set up as an object of ridicule by the purveyors of "love" who opposed him.

For the sake of his people he had put his own life at risk on many occasions over the years whilst attempting to subdue those forces of evil that affect the destinies of men. On each trip to the moon he had run the risk of being tempted to visit the house of a woman who was called "the wide crutch"—a self-conscious young lady whose habit it was to punish any man who laughed at her by tearing the entrails out of his belly and feeding them to her dogs. Nor was there a lousier job known to man than the one he had been expected to perform whenever the hunting was bad, for to appease the old crone who lived on the sea bed he had not only to survive a journey that was exceedingly hazardous, but to ingratiate himself in the company of that filthy, fingerless old hag, clean out

The Thule Eskimos' route lay north across frozen sea then along a frozen fjord. From there they climbed a frozen river in the lee of a huge moraine, and across this on to a glacier which led up to a windswept col at a height of 1,000 metres (3,000 feet). From there they careered down a cataract of ice which plunged in silent waves to the sea and when they had put 150 kilometres (90 miles) behind them they set up their new home.

her squalid house and comb the vermin from her hair.

The missionaries, of course, lived in the hope that their services to their fellow men would be duly rewarded in Heaven. Not so the *angákoqs*, for although the Eskimos believed that after death a soul may return to Earth and during the naming of a new-born child, slip into its body through the anus, they were rather vague about the relationship and seldom gave it much thought. Life was their main concern, and this for the most part they enjoyed so intensely that the prospect of a better deal in Heaven had not occurred to them. Their only fear was of things they encountered here on Earth that were malevolent or inexplicable, and it

had been the old man's unenviable job as a member of the native "clergy" to please or appease the world of spirits and so leave the hunters free to hunt. His function had been vital to the community— only he could make the catch plentiful and guide and protect them through the hazards of their daily lives.

As the *angákoq* he had possessed no official authority, for the Polar Eskimos were individualists—a society without chiefs or subordinates; a society without class, or cant, in which the only honour was the short-lived esteem of one's fellow men, and the only authority— the law of nature by which as predators all were bound. And yet, in a sense he had been their leader, and in a sense, the only man in his tribe who was a thinker.

Of course, he knew nothing about the NATO Alliance or the treaty between Denmark and the United States on the joint defence of Greenland. Nor did he know that to his north across the Arctic Ocean and beyond the place his people call the Navel of the Earth, there was another race of men as powerful as those he called the *Anaqaq* that had been left behind in his valley after the roaring birds had gone, or that they, the "Little Excrement", and their enemies the Russians who lived beyond the Pole, were in such fear of each other that in the name of self defence they were preparing for a holocaust in which all life on Earth was threatened with extinc-

By hitching up their dogs and turning away from the lights of Thule they were, they believed, reversing time and giving themselves a second chance to choose their destiny.

Drawings, opposite, top, and below, by the author.

How much time they had gained for themselves it is hard to say, for the northward march of the white race had not stopped at Thule. This remote, but no longer isolated, tribe soon found itself with a foot in both worlds. Although free to hunt to their hearts' content, they were dependent on the Danes for guns, ammunition, tobacco and tea and all the amenities of their new way of life for which they paid with skins.

tion. He knew nothing of the clash of ideologies between the East and West, or of the hatred and turmoil in the world, or of the great imbalance of poverty and wealth among the people who lived in the lands to his south. Even such basic concepts as war, and crime and original sin were beyond his comprehension, for he was an unsophisticated man.

In that summer of 1952 he had seen amphibious landings equal to four fully equipped combat divisions. He had seen supply convoys totalling 120 ships, and a construction force of no less than 13,000 men. He had seen and heard 300,000 tons of thundering machinery gouge the soul out of Pitufik valley and the dust settle less than ten weeks later on the biggest military installation in the world. He had seen his village overrun by sweet-smelling

men who in exchange for cans of food and small metal discs which they called "dimes" had taken the hunter's harpoons and whips.

But the old man had grown tired of the miracles he had seen and of his own reflected grin in the lenses of the cameras that had been pointed at him. He had grown tired of the noise; tired of the sight of fair-skinned men and of the glimpse of the future he had seen through the dark tunnel of 5,000 years which separated his people and their Stone-Age culture from those who, unable to function as men, had built and attached themselves like lice to the body of a machine.

Closing his eyes he remembered how once Pitufik had been a beautiful and very peaceful valley, soft-carpeted each summer with tiny flowers and alive with the song of birds and the sound of rushing streams. But its changing moods then were known only to the *Inuit*—the "real men". It would never be the same again, even though the sounds that flowed over him like a gentle breeze were the sounds of his

village—the same clutch of stone and turf dens that had for years been his home; for around him now the young hunters were discussing how much money they would get from the white men for their carvings, while the older men were lamenting that *Arnaquagssâq* would be offended by the presence of the strangers and would drive away the seals. He heard the sound of a slap and the piercing shriek of a crude woman's laugh, the murmur of young lovers in the skin tent just behind him and the laughter of the children down at the water's edge as they picked happily amongst the rubbish washed ashore by the last high tide. Each tin can to them was an exotic toy; each explosion in the valley further proof to their parents, if any were needed, that the American engineers were more powerful men than the Danish missionaries, who in turn were more powerful than the frail old man who sat slumped against a rock in shallow sleep while the heavy throbbing of the American base bored into his brain.

What is happening in the outside world the Eskimos can now find out at the flick of of a switch. Weather forecasts, personal messages, prayers and hymns for the pious traveller, country music for the middle-aged and pop for the teenage hunter—all given air space in their own language. And in the churches every Sunday they are reminded that their ancestors were born and died in sin.

Suddenly he was seized by a racking cramp which threatened to snap every muscle in his body. Those sitting near him could see him screaming but hear no sound. They could see his eyelids straining to separate as though the old man's mind was trying to escape from its darkness. In their terror they tried to edge away, but they could not move for fear they might miss the words that were now coming in surges and shaking his body in violent spasms, and with his eyes still tight shut and his black hair flying, he eventually burnt himself out and slumped in a crumpled heap.

He never fully recovered and a few months later he died; but the advice he had given his people had gone too close to their hearts to be ignored, and they had slid away silently on the black ice of autumn, their dogs and sledges moving like shadows out of the glow of artificial light which spread out across the frozen sea from the aluminium city the Americans call Thule, and into a darkness full of unseen shapes.

Of course, for a migrating tribe to survive it is not essential that the "grass is always greener on the other side of the hill"—it is essential only that its leader is convinced that

The Eskimos now have boats but only the old folk can remember what life was like without them.

this is so. But what few leaders there had been among the Polar Eskimos had, by 1952, all died or been degraded. They could not even look to their folk heroes for inspiration or example, for even Kritlaq, the greatest *angákoq* of them all, whose spiritual reconnaissance flights had led to the last migration of Eskimos from Baffin Island in the Canadian Arctic to the Thule District of north-west Greenland, and who is said to have guided his people through the polar night by the light of the flames which shot out of his head, had become so homesick on reaching his "promised land" in 1864 that within a few years he had set out on his return. What hope then was there for the Thule tribe that was now spreading out in panic from beneath the jackboot that was about to crush them?

The short answer is, they thrived. In fact, it is hard to see on looking back that it could have been otherwise, for they had run straight into the open arms of a benign Danish Administration which had closed around them instantly in a fat, motherly embrace so warm and comforting, so protective and gentle compared with the endless struggle for survival which their tribe had always known, that it was several years before even the most independent among them twisted their mouths off the breast that fed them to curse it because it was white. And by that time they had changed.

And while the old men in the summer dream of living out their lives as hunters . . .

. . . the young long for the chance to break free from their isolation and fly south to the "real" world.

The hunters now have motor boats, their wives now take the pill and their children play at killing men like other normal kids. And they all live in houses with double-glazed windows and coal fires with ovens in which they bake bread, and their frozen smalls and floral sheets and fashionable shirts flap stiffly on the washing lines on the first day of each week. In fact, they have become civilized, for all but a few can now read and write and they can all now count their change, and they all smoke and all drink and all beat their wives and all go to church when the flag smacks the wind and the weather is no good for hunting.

But they have failed on one count to integrate—and that weakness is their strength. For they are as hunters superior they think, and disguise with a smile the scowl of contempt which protects the Eskimo's vulnerable pride from the white man's profound conceit.

How long can they survive—will they still be driving their dogs and hunting in the traditional way thirty years from now?

The answer is in the tide of events that affects the outside world, for these people are no longer independent. To their south live 4,000 million people —they themselves number only 500. Their only exports are skins and pelts of the arctic fox and a boycott on these or a mere whim of fashion could tip the scales of survival against them, for the Polar Eskimo will not accept charity. They earned their first reprieve by escaping and it is my belief that a few at least will do the same again.

ACKNOWLEDGMENTS

Arktisk Institut, Charlottenlund, Denmark: pp. 15, 29, 35, 41, 42, 57 (bottom), 94 (bottom), 98 (top). British Museum: 105 (top), 108 (both). Danish National Museum: 30 (all). The Danish Tourist Board: 109 (top, photograph by Peter Juul). The Herbert Collection: 2, 4, 6, 9, 10, 11, 21, 22, 25, 26 (photograph by John Petersen), 28, 31, 32, 34 (both, photographs by K. Rasmussen), 36, 37 (both), 38, 39, 40 (bottom right), 42 (top and middle), 44, 46 (middle), 47, 48 (both), 49, 50, 51, 52 (both), 53, 54, 55, 56 (upper), 57 (upper), 58, 59, 60, 62 (both), 64, 65, 66 (bottom), 68 (right), 70, 72–73, 74 (both), 75 (all), 76 (all), 77 (top), 80, 82 (all), 83 (both), 84, 85 (both), 86, 88 (both), 89, 90 (both), 91, 92, 93 (both), 96 (all), 97, 98 (two lower), 99, 100 (both), 104 (both), 107 (top), 110 (two top left and middle), 114, 116 (top), 117, 118 (both), 119, 120, 120–121, 122, 123 (top), 124 (both), 125 (both). Hudson's Bay Co.: 105 (bottom), 107 (bottom, photograph by Franklin Arbuckle).

National Film Board of Canada (Netsilik Eskimo Series): 13, 19, 56 (bottom), 66 (upper), 68 (left), 77 (bottom), 81 (both), 123 (bottom). Pressehuset: 27 (above), 63 (photographs by Gunvor Jørgsholm). Rolf Muller: 79, 102, 111 (both), 112 (middle and bottom). Royal Danish Embassy, London: 78 (below). Royal Danish Ministry for Foreign Affairs: 27 (bottom), 46 (top), 106 (bottom), 109 (bottom), 110 (top right), 112 (top), 113 (both, photographs by Morgens S. Koch), 116 (bottom). University of Alaska Archives: 16 (Gertrude Lusk Collection), 24, 40, 43 (Kromer Family Collection), 69 (Gertrude Lusk Collection), 94 (Guy F. Cameron Collection), 95 (Gertrude Lusk Collection), 106 (middle, Barrett Willoughby Archives). The Whaling Museum, New Bedford, Mass.: 106 (top).

The publishers are grateful to Mr Michael Shand of the University of Glasgow for drawing the maps on pages 8, 12, 14, 17 and 72.

Cover and endpapers: Wally Herbert.

FURTHER READING

Ames, Gerald, and Wyler Rose. *The Story of the Ice Age* New York: Harper and Row, 1956.

Balikci, A. *The Netsilik Eskimo* Ottawa: National Film Board of Canada, 1970.

Bandi, H. G. *Eskimo Prehistory* London: Methuen & Co., 1969.

Birket-Smith, K. *Eskimos* New York: Crown Publishing Co., 1971.

Bringle, Mary. *Eskimos (A First Book)* New York: Franklin Watts, 1973.

Bruemmer, F. *Seasons of the Eskimos* Toronto: McClelland & Stewart, 1971.

— *Encounters with Arctic Animals* Toronto: McGraw-Hill, 1972.

— *The Arctic* Montreal: Infocor Ltd, 1975.

Butler, F. F. and the Marquis of Lorne. *Bering Sea Controversy* facsimile edition. Seattle: Shorey Publications, 1892.

Carpenter, Edmund, ed. *The Story of Comock the Eskimo* New York: Simon & Schuster, 1968.

Chance, N. A. *The Eskimo of North Alaska* New York: Holt Rinehart & Winston Inc., 1966.

Claiborne, Robert. *First Americans* Emergence of Man Series. New York: Time-Life Books, 1973.

Coy, Harold. *Man Comes to America* Boston: Little, Brown, 1973.

Erngaard, E. *Greenland Then and Now* Copenhagen: Lademann Ltd, 1972.

Field, Edward, ed. *Eskimo Songs and Stories: Collected by Knud Rasmussen on the Fifth Thule Expedition* New York: Delacorte Press, 1973.

Flaherty, Robert, dir. *Nanook of the North* (film) Paramount, 1922. London: Abelard Schuman, 1971.

Freuchen, P. *Book of the Eskimos* New York: Fawcett World Library, 1961.

Freuchen, P. and Salomonsen, F. *The Arctic Year* London: Jonathan Cape, 1959.

George, Jane Craighead. *Julie of the Wolves* New York: Harper & Row, 1972. Dramatized on Newbery Records, 1973.

Gillham, Charles E. *Beyond the Clapping Mountains* New York: Macmillan, 1964.

Glubok, Shirley. *Art of the Eskimo* New York: Harper & Row, 1964.

Herbert, Wally. *Polar Deserts* Glasgow: Collins, 1971. New York: Franklin Watts, 1971.

Herbert, Wally. *Across the Top of the World: The Last Journey on Earth* New York: G. P. Putnam's Sons, 1971.

Houston, James A. *Tikta'liktak: An Eskimo Legend* New York: Harcourt Brace Jovanovich, 1965.

— *Wolf Run: A Caribou Eskimo Tale* New York: Harcourt Brace Jovanovich, 1971.

— ed. *Songs of the Dream People: Chants & Images from the Indians, and Eskimos of North America* New York: Atheneum, 1972.

Jenness, Aylette. *Dwellers of the Tundra: Life in an Alaskan Village* New York: Macmillan, 1970.

Jenness, D. *The People of Twilight* new edition 1967. Chicago: University of Chicago Press, 1928.

— *Eskimo Administration* (5 vols) Montreal: Arctic Institute of North America, 1962–68.

Macdonald, R. St J. ed. *The Arctic Frontier* Toronto: University of Toronto Press, 1966.

MacNeish, Richard, ed. *Early Man in America: Readings From Scientific American* San Francisco: W. H. Freeman, 1973.

Malaurie, J. *The Last Kings of Thule* London: George Allen & Unwin Ltd, 1956.

Mary-Rousselière, Guy. *Beyond the High Hills: A Book of Eskimo Poems* Cleveland: Collins World, 1971.

May, Julian. *They Lived in the Ice Age* New York: Holiday House, 1967.

Ministry for Greenland. *Greenland past and present* Copenhagen: Henriksen, 1971.

Mirsky, Jeanette. *To the Arctic: The Story of Northern Exploration from Earliest Times to the Present* Chicago: University of Chicago Press, 1970.

Mowat, F. *Canada North* Toronto: McClelland & Stewart, 1967.

— *Curse of the Viking Grave* Boston: Little, Brown, 1956.

— *People of the Deer* London: Readers Union, 1954.

Pitseolak. *Pitseolak: Pictures Out of My Life* Dorothy Eber, ed. Seattle: University of Washington Press, 1972.

Rasmussen, Knud J. *Across Arctic America: Narrative of the Fifth Thule Expedition* Reprint of 1927 edn Westport, Conn.: Greenwood Press, 1968.

Rasmussen, K. *People of the Polar North* London: Macmillan, 1908.

Rink, H. *Danish Greenland, its people and products* (reprint) 1974. London: C. Hurst & Co., 1972.

Rudenko, S. I. *Ancient Culture of the Bering Sea & the Eskimo Problem* Henry N. Michael, ed.; Paul Tolstoy, tr. Toronto: University of Toronto Press, 1961.

Spencer, R. F. *The North Alaskan Eskimo* Washington D.C.: Smithsonian Institution Press, 1959.

Steensel, M. van, ed. *People of Light and Dark* Ottawa: The Queen's Printer, 1966.

Stefansson, V. *My life with the Eskimos* new edition 1951. New York: Macmillan, 1913.

Swinton, G. *Sculpture of the Eskimos* London: C. Hurst & Co., 1972.

Wilkinson, D. *The Arctic Coast* N.S.L. Natural Science of Canada Ltd, 1970.

Wilson, Carter. *On Firm Ice* New York: Crowell, 1970.

INDEX

Figures in italics indicate illustrations